UNLOCKING
8 FIGURES

UNLOCKING
8 FIGURES

THE ROADMAP TO $10M

HUNTER BALLEW

ISBN: 979-8-89316-623-1 (Paperback)
ISBN: 979-8-89316-622-4 (Ebook)

CONTENTS

INTRODUCTION

As I reflect on my journey from a firefighter who wanted more out of life, to what most would consider a successful entrepreneur, one truth stands out above all others: the growth of your business is intrinsically tied to your growth as a leader. This book isn't just about strategies and tactics for business success; it's about the personal development required to become the kind of leader capable of steering an organization to eight figures and beyond. It's about facing your own challenges head-on and continuously evolving to meet the demands of a growing organization.

My path to leadership began in the structured environments of the Marine Corps and the fire service. These experiences laid the foundation for my understanding of leadership, but not always in the ways you might expect. Some of the most impactful lessons came from observing poor leadership. Unfortunately, more times than not, seeing someone do something the way you think it *shouldn't* be done is what helps you form your own style of leadership, rather than vice versa.

These experiences taught me an invaluable lesson: sometimes, the best leadership education comes from observing what not to do. It wasn't about mimicking good examples, but rather about resolving to avoid the pitfalls I witnessed and creating a leadership style that inspired and uplifted others.

Most of what I saw were so called "leaders" who demanded respect and didn't earn it. Since stepping away from both the USMC and the fire department in 2015 I've striven to be a leader people want to link arms with.

This book is written with one goal in mind; help you grow beyond 8 figures while having fun.

While the large majority of this book will be filled with practical steps and my real life experience, I want to quickly share how I gained this knowledge that I'm going to share. I'd love to be the next business expert, but the reality is I'm not that smart. I just work hard and don't quit.

Here's a quick glance at my 'resume:'

- Married with two kiddos.
- Nine figures in revenue.
- Multiple eight-figure years across my portfolio.
- Annual conference, RoofCON, with 5K-plus attendees and hundreds of vendors.
- Partner in RepCard app with 125K-plus users and millions of cards sent.
- Acquisition of Roofing.com.
- Exited Cornerstone Construction for $48 million and repurchased it at a fraction.
- Millions in real estate.
- Created the Fearless 44 Challenge with thousands of participants worldwide.
- Created the Revolt Community, which serves thousands of business owners.
- Author of *Wall Street Journal* number-one bestseller: *Make It Count.*
- Spoke on stages with John C. Maxwell, Ed Mylett, Mike Tyson, Tim Tebow, and more.

Now, I didn't list any of those accomplishments to brag. To be honest, my list of failures is much longer. It's simply to give context to why I'm writing this book and show you what's possible if you think you're not qualified.

I grew up in a small town and only made it out of high school because my 12th grade English teacher cut me some slack and passed me. I finished 189 out of 212 and have always had to do things the hard way myself before I learned. Both my parents were drug addicts and I didn't know what was possible until I began to invest in myself. If I can find success, you can too.

Are you ready to learn strategies and tactics for business success? Are you ready to undergo the personal development required to become the kind of leader capable of steering an organization to eight figures and beyond? I hope this book is the first step for you. I'm rooting for you the whole way. Let's get started!

CHAPTER 1

The Leader I Must Become

As I've grown in my leadership journey, I've identified several traits that I believe are crucial for any leader aiming to scale a business to eight figures and beyond.

1.   Accountability:

In the early days of Cornerstone Construction, I can remember not only when we missed our mark on sales, but also who was to blame: myself. Sure, it would have been easy to point fingers at individual team members, but I knew that as the leader, the ultimate responsibility was mine.

As John C. Maxwell said, "A good leader takes a little more than his share of the blame and a little less than his share of credit." This quote resonates deeply with me because I've learned firsthand the power of accountability in leadership; that accountability starts at the top. So, I asked myself, *What can I do differently to keep this from happening in the future?*

I looked over the prior week's schedule. *I, and the leadership team, could have hosted more regular meetings for training and role-play to help the sales team achieve their numbers*—and that's exactly what we did.

We made accountability a "cornerstone" of our company culture, and we instituted weekly meetings where team members could openly discuss challenges and seek support. We even celebrated when people recognized and owned up to mistakes so that they could be used as opportunities for the rest of the team to learn.

Over time, this culture of accountability became a key driver of our growth and success. Before you can hold your team accountable, you must hold yourself to the highest standard.

2. Discipline:

In the words of Zig Ziglar, "It was character that got us out of bed, commitment that moved us into action, and discipline that enabled us to follow through." This quote aligns perfectly with a saying I share often to those around me: "You get to choose – the pain of discipline or the pain of regret."

It sucks to get up early in the morning. It sucks to bypass the ice cream when you want another scoop. It sucks to go on the run. A lot of things are *just not fun* when it comes to discipline. But when you skip the pain of discipline, you'll experience the pain of regret. Regret because you're overweight, because you have health problems, because you have heart problems, because you can't run with your kid at their soccer game. You're going to have pain regardless. It will either be pain of discipline in the moment, or pain of regret down the road.

The importance of discipline was driven home for me in a deeply personal way through my grandpa's story. My "Pops" was a central figure in my life. He was the one who took me under his wing when things were tough at home, the one who taught me the value of hard work as we rode around in his old blue truck, taking care of his landscaping customers.

But he had one habit he couldn't shake – smoking. He started when he was fourteen and continued even after being diagnosed and beating cancer during my freshman year of high school. Despite the wake-up call that cancer provided, he hadn't built the discipline to quit.

Ultimately, this lack of discipline cost him his life, and it cost our family precious time with him. Now, when I visit my Mimi's house with my kids, Turner and Fields, it kills me to see them sit in his old chair without him there. He wasn't at my wedding and didn't get to be there to root me on through all my business ventures and big life events. His choice – his lack of discipline – robbed him, and us, of those priceless moments.

This experience crystallized for me the real-world implications of discipline. It's not just about personal success or achievement – it's about being there for the people who matter most, about living long enough and well enough to see your impact ripple out through generations.

In business and in life, discipline might be uncomfortable in the moment. It might mean making tough choices, putting in extra hours, or saying no to tempting distractions. But these short-term discomforts are small in comparison to the long-term pain of regret, of opportunities missed, of potential unfulfilled.

This lesson has shaped my approach to leadership profoundly. I strive to model discipline in all areas – in how I manage my time, in how I approach challenges, in how I take care of my health. And I work to instill this value in my team, always reminding them that discipline is the bridge from goals to accomplishments.

3. Vision:

In my experience, vision is what separates true leaders from managers. It's about seeing possibilities where others see obstacles, about painting a picture of a future so effectively that people are willing to work tirelessly to make it a reality. As Jim Rohn says, "Leadership is the challenge to be something more than average," and to be more than average, you need a clear, compelling vision that inspires others to reach beyond their perceived limitations.

When I started Cornerstone Construction, my vision wasn't just about building a successful roofing company. It was about creating an organization that could change the lives of our employees, our customers, and our community. I envisioned a company that would not only provide excellent service but give back to the community and provide opportunities for growth and development to everyone involved.

This vision became our north star. It guided our decisions, inspired our team, and attracted like-minded individuals who wanted to be part of something bigger than themselves. It's what pushed us to grow from $1 million in revenue in our first year to over $15 million a couple of years later.

But how? Understand that having a vision isn't enough—you need to be able to communicate what you aspire to achieve in an effective manner. For example, I knew my vision for Cornerstone was big enough to inspire and meaningful enough to create lasting motivation, but I needed to make sure it was also clear enough to follow. This is why I came up with the 10-10-1: 10 locations, $10 million per location, $1 million given back to the community through Cornerstone Kids. To this day, I can remember standing in front of my team, sharing my vision, and watching the excitement in their eyes as they grasped the magnitude of what we were setting out to accomplish, as they made it their vision too.

4. Empathy:

You may have a great vision, and you may have your team members completely bought in, but, as Craig Groeschel says, "People don't follow vision. They follow people who have vision," and here is the importance of connecting with your team on a human level.

Making that connection with your colleagues as a leader is about more than just being nice—it's about truly understanding and valuing the experiences, feelings, and perspectives of those you lead. It's about creating an environment where people feel seen, heard, and appreciated. It's about expressing empathy.

For example, one of your top performers starts showing up late and missing deadlines. Your instinctual response is probably going to be frustration. Instead of immediately reprimanding him, be slow to speak and quick to listen. Have a private conversation and try to understand what's going on. When people feel understood and supported, they're more engaged, more productive, and more committed to the team's success.

This is because empathy is a powerful tool when it comes to supporting our team through their difficult times. It allows us to build trust, foster loyalty to you and the rest of the team, and ultimately drive better business results while accomplishing tasks that need to be done.

5. Resilience:

The path to success is never smooth, and how you handle setbacks and failures will largely determine your success. As John Maxwell puts it, "The difference between average people and achieving people is their perception of, and response to, failure." Resilience may be one of the most critical traits for any leader, especially one aiming to scale a business to eight figures.

I remember a moment early in my entrepreneurial journey that tested my resilience to its limits. I had left my steady job at the fire department to chase my dreams, and felt confident in the $60,000 I had saved up as a safety net. So, I threw myself into learning everything I could about business—buying courses, joining mastermind groups, working with consultants, etc.

Before I knew it, I had blown through all of our savings. I still remember the sick feeling in my stomach when my wife told me we were out of cash.

It would have been easy to give up at that point, to crawl back to my old job with my tail between my legs.

But that wasn't an option for me. I knew I had to find a way through it.

It's easy to be discouraged, but as leaders, we must remember that "the pressure is a privilege." So I embraced the hard times, doubled down on my efforts, pushed harder than ever before, and got creative with ways to generate income. It wasn't easy, but it showed me that I had the strength to weather storms and come out stronger on the other side. It taught me the true meaning of resilience, which has served me well throughout my business journey.

Whether it was dealing with difficult clients, navigating market downturns, or facing unexpected challenges, that ability to bounce back, to keep pushing forward even when things got tough, has been crucial to my team's success, and yes, I do mean my whole team. As a leader, your resilience doesn't just affect you—it sets the tone for your entire organization. Because when your team sees you facing challenges head-on and maintaining a positive attitude in the face of adversity, it inspires them to do the same.

6. Problem-solving:

In my experience, strong problem-solving skills are what separate good leaders from great ones. Effective problem-solving is about asking the right questions, gathering the right information, and being able to think creatively to find not just any solution, but the right solution. As a leader, your job isn't to have all the answers – it's to create an environment where problems can be identified, analyzed, and solved effectively.

The mindset you cultivate as a leader plays a crucial role in your effectiveness and the success of your organization. "Life isn't happening to you; it's happening for you." Wisdom shared by Tony Robbins has been transformative in my leadership journey. It's about seeing challenges as opportunities for growth rather than obstacles to success.

This mindset shift was particularly powerful for me in overcoming the challenges of my upbringing. Growing up with parents who struggled with addiction, I carried shame and guilt for years. I didn't know how I would create my own legacy, separate from the circumstances I was born into.

Overcoming this mindset was a long, challenging process. It required me to reframe my experiences, to see how they had shaped me in positive ways – giving me resilience, empathy, and a drive to succeed. I had to learn to see my background not as a limitation, but as a unique perspective that could inform my leadership and help me connect with others facing their own struggles.

This journey taught me the power of perspective in leadership. When you can reframe challenges as opportunities, it not only changes how you approach problems, but it also inspires your team to do the same.

Another game-changer for me came from Jocko Willink's approach of responding, "Good" when facing challenges. When team members come to you with issues, the response should be, "Good." Why? Because it's an opportunity for growth.

Sales are down this month. *Good, a reason to train more!*

Our key player is resigning. *Good, an opportunity for the right person to step up!*

A customer is mad. *Good, a chance to make it right and win a customer for life!*

Remember, it's all happening *for* you, not *to* you.

After contracting malaria from a trip to Africa in 2023, I was cooped up in a hospital bed and frustrated. My health had taken a beating—thirty pounds of muscle gone in a month—and I was going stir-crazy wanting to get back to work. I was grateful that many people reached out with sympathy, but one call I received from my mentor and former chief at the fire department, Ricky Williams, held a much different tune.

In fact, he skipped the whole sympathy bit and asked, "What are you learning from this?"

This simple question helped shift my mindset to focus on the positives even in the face of significant setbacks.

Concepts of Leadership

John C. Maxwell's "Law of the Lid" states that an organization's potential is directly related to the ability of its leader. This concept made me realize that to grow my business I first needed to grow myself.

It's why I've invested over $1 million in my own personal development through books, coaches, consultants, events, and mastermind groups. This might seem like a lot, but I view it as an investment in the future of my businesses and my ability to impact others, and an investment for all of my team members.

I remember joining a high-level mastermind group that cost $60,000 a year. It's a significant investment for anyone, but gaining insights on my challenges and learning from the experiences of these successful entrepreneurs turned out to be invaluable. In one fifteen-minute conversation with another member, I learned about a tax strategy that ended up saving my business hundreds of thousands of dollars. But more than that, being part of that group expanded my vision of what was possible and pushed me to think bigger about my goals and the impact they'd have.

The business world is constantly evolving, and as leaders, we need to evolve with it. Whether it's through reading books, attending conferences, working with coaches, or simply seeking out conversations with people who challenge your thinking, ongoing education is crucial for any leader who wants to stay effective and relevant.

Leadership often requires making difficult decisions that can have far-reaching consequences, which makes staying true to your values, even when it comes at a significant cost, one of the most challenging aspects of leadership.

For instance, one of Cornerstone Construction's non-negotiable values is integrity, and we make this clear to our customers, our team, and our partners. At one point, we discovered that a leader in one of our markets was compromising on this value. Despite the financial implications, we made the decision to shut down that entire market. It was a painful decision that impacted many people, but it was necessary to maintain the integrity of our organization.

This experience taught me that your values are only as strong as your willingness to uphold them, even when it hurts. It also reinforced the importance of clearly communicating these values and ensuring that everyone in a leadership position is fully aligned with them. When you sacrifice values at the leadership level, you compromise the integrity and lose trust at all other levels within your company.

Another example stems from Chip and Joanna Gaines, the founders of the Magnolia brand, and the stars of HGTV's *Fixer Upper*. The show was HGTV's highest rated program, attracting millions of viewers and bringing in substantial revenue. At the height of its popularity in 2017, they made a significant decision to end their hit TV show with HGTV.

Chip Gaines said in an interview, "We gave everything we had to this show—the beautiful homes and those sweet families—but this just felt like the right time to catch our breath for a bit."

Then Joanna added, "We really want to focus on this break and take a step back to let this all soak in. Regardless of what the future holds, we are hopeful for what God has for us and our family in this next season."

This decision wasn't just about taking a break; it was about aligning their work with one of their core values, family. When the Gaineses realized that the demanding filming schedule was taking a toll on their family life, they chose family time over continued fame and financial gain from the show. This move, while risky, ultimately allowed them to refocus on their family and build their Magnolia empire in a way that better aligned with their personal values.

Sometimes, staying true to your core values means making difficult decisions that might seem counterintuitive from a purely business perspective. When really, in the long run, these decisions can lead to greater fulfillment and even greater success by strengthening your organization, and creating a culture of trust and integrity that attracts like-minded employees and customers, ultimately contributing to your sustainable growth.

To help you put these leadership concepts into practice, I've developed three powerful exercises: *Embedded*, *Defined*, and *The Six Bricks*. These tools will help you clarify your values, define your mission, and set concrete goals for personal and professional growth.

1. Embedded:

The *Embedded* exercise is about creating Life Laws that not only *you* live by, but your spouse and children as well. These laws are the core principles that guide your decisions and actions as a family.

To create your Life Laws, begin by brainstorming. Sit down and write all of the things that are really important to you, everything you can think of. Don't worry about the length of your list – we will condense it in the next step. Ask yourself some questions: What do you stand for? As a man or woman? As a husband or wife? Father or mother? As a business owner? What words come to mind? Write down everything you can think of.

Once you've finished your list, you'll see that some words fit into the same category as other words. For example, number one on my family's Life Laws is "Man of Integrity." Honesty was another word on our list. When we thought about it, we decided that honesty can fall under "Man of Integrity" because to be a man of integrity, you have to be honest.

My family and I were able to whittle down our list to five Life Laws:

1. Man of Integrity
2. Value People
3. Positive Attitude
4. Purpose-Driven
5. Chase Greatness

To reinforce these Life Laws, we create mantras—concise, memorable sayings that solidify each principle. For "Man of Integrity," we say, "Do the right thing even when nobody's watching." This mantra encourages us to maintain our principles regardless of where we are or who's watching. It might be tempting to ignore a piece of trash in a park when no one's around, but a person of integrity will leave the place better than they found it. A couple of other examples of mantras that support our fifth Life Law, "Chase Greatness", is "against average" or "me versus me". This reminds us to strive for excellence, to push beyond mediocrity, and never settle for less than our best. When coming up with your Life Law mantras, remember that these mantras serve as daily reminders, helping us internalize and act upon our Life Laws in practical, everyday situations.

After Life Laws and mantras, the third component of the *Embedded* exercise is actions. These are the concrete steps we take to embody our Life Laws and mantras. Let's look at some examples in my own family:

1. Man of Integrity: This involves actions like picking up trash even when no one's watching, and consistently doing the right thing.
2. Value People: We demonstrate this by helping others, like assisting someone with car trouble or buying a meal for a stranger. It's about engaging positively with people— conversing, showing genuine interest in others' well-being, and valuing everyone, from the highest paid person in the room to the lowest.

3. Positive Attitude: This is particularly important for our five-year-old son. We encourage maintaining a good attitude and a positive outlook, always remembering to be grateful for the life that we have.

4. Purpose-Driven: Being able to explain why we do what we do is key for this. We're able to convey our message to anyone and everyone at a moment's notice.

5. Chase Greatness: This manifests in pushing ourselves a little harder each time—doing one more rep at the gym, running faster, or going the extra mile in our endeavors.

To recap, the *Embedded* exercise consists of three key elements:

1. Life Laws: our core principles.
2. Mantras: short, memorable phrases that reinforce these principles.
3. Actions: specific behaviors that bring our Life Laws and mantras to life.

By aligning these three elements, we create a powerful framework for living our values every day.

2. Defined:

The second exercise we'll explore is called *Defined*. While *Embedded* focuses on the values we build our lives around, *Defined* is about articulating your life mission.

In this exercise, you'll define your life's purpose in a concise, memorable statement. Ideally, this should be a single simple sentence that not only captures what you want to accomplish in your life, but can be memorized and recited with ease. For example, my life mission statement is, "I will develop millions of leaders that go on to impact billions of lives."

The power of a well-defined life mission statement lies in its clarity and simplicity. It becomes a touchstone for all your actions and choices, ensuring that you're always moving toward your ultimate purpose.

To create your life mission, I recommend focusing on three crucial elements:

1. **Who**: Identify the specific group of people you want to serve.

In my case, it's leaders—specifically the driven 1 percent who are hungry for growth and want more out of life. I'm passionate about pouring into and helping these individuals develop into more impactful leaders.

For you, it might be different. Who is your target audience? Who do you feel called to help or impact? Is it underprivileged children? Athletes? Your church community? People from a specific country? Survivors of abuse? The key here is to pinpoint the community that resonates with your passions and values. Who is the 'who' for you? Who do you feel drawn to serve?

Take some time to reflect on this. Your 'who' forms the foundation of your life mission, so it's crucial to choose a group that truly ignites your passion and sense of purpose.

2. **How**: Determine your method of impact.

In my case, I develop people as leaders. My goal is to help them grow as leaders so they can, in turn, reach and impact more people.

What about you? What is your approach? How are you going to help them? What's the vehicle for your impact?

Your 'how' doesn't need to be complex. The only thing it needs to be is in alignment with your 'who.' It can be that you want to take underprivileged kids fishing. It could be that you want to give back to the local wrestling team. It could be that you want to teach dance classes. The key is to choose a method that feels authentic to you and effectively serves your target group. Your 'how' should be something you're excited about and can sustain over time.

3.   **Wow**: The wow factor.

We have the 'who,' the 'how,' and lastly, we have the 'wow.' The 'wow' factor puts a tangible, quantifiable dimension on your life mission. It's an ambitious, yet achievable goal that you can measure your progress against.

So, how do you define your 'wow'? First, choose a number that represents significant impact. Make sure it's specific and measurable, while also being both ambitious and attainable. Your 'wow' factor might involve hundreds, thousands, or millions—whatever feels both inspiring and achievable for you. The key is to make it measurable.

For me, the 'wow' is that I want to develop millions of leaders to impact billions of lives. I don't just say, "Yep, I'm helping people!" I'm asking myself, *Am I helping enough people to reach my goal before I'm no longer in this world?* This allows me to assess whether I'm on track to reach my specific goal within my lifetime.

So to recap, my 'who' are the leaders, my 'how' is that I want to develop them as leaders, and my 'wow' is that those leaders will go on to impact billions of lives.

Once you've defined your own specific 'who,' 'how,' and 'wow,' combine these elements into a concise, powerful one-line statement. This becomes your life mission—a clear, memorable guide for your actions and decisions that should inspire you and provide a clear direction for your efforts.

3. The Six Bricks:

This is the last exercise to complete the trio. First we have *Embedded*, then *Defined*, now *The Six Bricks*.

The Six Bricks exercise is a goal-setting framework covering six key areas of life:

1. Health
2. Wealth
3. Faith
4. Growth
5. Relationships
6. Legacy

When you think about *The Six Bricks*, imagine you're building your legacy where each brick you accomplish gets stacked up, one on top of the other. Now, ask yourself: Do you want your legacy to be a little storage shed out back, or do you want it to be the Taj Mahal? More importantly, are you aiming to leave behind a massive legacy that continues to impact people long after you're gone?

I ask because for me, legacy isn't about money or inheritance. It's simply the impact you make on people after you're gone, whether they know your name or not. So what do you want your legacy to be? I firmly believe these six areas of life—what I call *The Six Bricks*—are areas we should focus on improving every single day if we want our legacy to grow beyond material things.

So, where do you stand right now in each of these six areas: Health, Wealth, Faith, Growth, Relationships, and Legacy? For each of these bricks, score yourself from 1 to 100.

HEALTH

THE⑥BRICKS
—— REVOLT ——

1 TO 100 RATING:

ACTION PLAN:

TARGET:

DEADLINE:

REASON:

CONSEQUENCE:

EXCUSE:

ACCOUNTABILITY PARTNER:

Finished with your evaluation?

Great, let's address the eight key components to *The Six Bricks*: Rating, Target, Deadline, Reason, Consequence, Excuse, Accountability Partner and Action Plan - in that order.

Rating - Now, because you have already graded yourself, you know your current rating. So, what's left? A simple goal: increase your rating.

Target - But how do you do that? Well, you start with a target. Let's take health as an example. If I'm at 20 percent body fat, my target might be to get down to 15 percent. Boom! That's my target.

Deadline - The next question you might be asking is, "How much time am I going to give myself to hit that target? Weeks? Months? Years?" You've got to have a deadline. Always. Without a deadline, it's just a wish, not an attainable goal. So put a date on that target. When are you going to make it happen? I typically have quarterly and annual targets.

Reason - After you've established your target and deadline, you'll write down your reason. Your 'why' is what's going to keep you going when things get tough.

Consequence - What happens if you don't hit your target? And don't tell me there's no consequence. That's BS. You wouldn't set the target if there wasn't something at stake. So, be honest with yourself here. Think deep, not just surface-level. If you don't hit your health goals, the consequence could be that you won't be able to walk your daughter down the aisle. Or that you won't be around to play with your grandchildren.

Excuse - This part is crucial: list your excuses. What's that go-to excuse you know you're going to use when it's time to put in the work? For health, it might be, "I'm too tired," or, "I don't have time." Write it down. Get it out in the open. Because when you see that excuse coming, you can shut it down before it derails you.

Accountability Partner - This is where having an accountability partner comes in. Who's going to keep you on track? Who's going to call you out when you start slacking? Remember, this isn't just about wishing for things to change—it's about taking action to crush your goal. So get specific, get real, and get yourself a true accountability partner.

Action Plan - Lastly, develop an action plan for how you are going to achieve the target by your deadline. Remember, "failing to plan is planning to fail." What do you need to do to hit this target?

Not only should you work through *The Six Bricks*, but I suggest you walk your family and team through it, too. Find out what drives them, help them achieve it, and the reward will come full circle.

Questioning Leadership

As you work on developing your leadership skills, consider these essential questions:

1. **How can you assess and improve your leadership skills?**

Self-awareness is crucial here and I'd consider it one of the most important leadership skills that a leader should have. If you're not self-aware, it's hard to be a good leader because you're not analyzing where you need improvement. You're looking at your wins, not your losses, failures, or how you can improve on serving your team. I'll touch on this more later, but allowing your people to give you feedback is extremely important.

I used to think I was a great communicator until I received some feedback from my team. They told me that while I was great at articulating our vision, I often failed to provide clear, actionable directions. This was hard to hear, but it was invaluable. It led me to work on my communication skills, and focus on providing more specific guidance while checking for understanding. It's something I realize I have to continually work on.

2. What daily practices can help build leadership traits?

Consistent small actions can lead to significant growth over time. Consider investing in yourself through going to events, reading books (I have a list of recommended books at the end of this chapter to get you started), hiring a coach, or joining a mastermind. Then go the extra mile and get your hands dirty by getting involved in the business again.

While I am a believer in hiring people smarter than you, so that you don't have to get your hands dirty, occasionally it is necessary to be involved. By doing this, you not only see where your company is at a baseline level but you learn where systems and processes are broken, which will give you a deeper understanding of how your team is operating.

3. What traits are essential for effective leadership?

Here are my *Seven Traits of the Greats*:

- Self-Awareness: Understand your strengths, weaknesses, and impact on others.
- Selfless Servant: Focus on the growth and well-being of your team and community.
- Positive Attitude: Consistently have a positive mindset and radiate positivity through the team to keep energy and momentum up.

- Legacy Focused: Think long term and consider the lasting impact of your actions.
- Belief in Others: See and nurture the potential in those around you. This is extremely important in inspiring others and pulling the best out of them so that they hit their next level. You must believe in them more than they believe in themselves.
- Relentless: When everyone else is ready to give up, you have full belief you will find a way. You are laser focused and never complacent.
- Decisive: Know how to analyze risk quickly so that you can make necessary decisions.

Leadership is not about perfection—it's about progress, which requires leveraging the strengths, ideas, and efforts of your entire team, not just achieving business goals. Every day presents new opportunities to apply these principles, learn from your experiences, and refine your leadership approach.

Becoming the leader your business needs is an ongoing journey of growth, self-reflection, and deliberate action. The traits, mindsets, and practices we've explored in this chapter form the foundation of effective leadership, but they're just the beginning. Real growth happens when you consistently apply these concepts in your daily life and business operations.

As you continue reading, keep in mind that your growth as a leader directly impacts the potential of your organization. By committing to continuous improvement and maintaining a legacy-focused mindset, you're not just working toward an eight-figure business—you're laying the groundwork for lasting, meaningful impact.

Remember:

1. The growth of your business is intrinsically tied to your growth as a leader.
2. Accountability, discipline, vision, empathy, resilience, and problem-solving are crucial traits for scaling a business to eight figures and beyond.
3. Cultivate a mindset that sees challenges as opportunities for growth rather than obstacles to success.
4. Continuous learning and personal development are essential investments for effective leadership.
5. Stay true to your core values, even when it comes at a significant cost.
6. Use the *Embedded, Defined*, and *The Six Bricks* exercises to clarify your values, define your mission, and set concrete goals for personal and professional growth.
7. Assess and improve your leadership skills regularly, practice self-awareness, and be open to feedback from your team.
8. Your growth as a leader directly impacts the potential of your organization, so commit to continuous improvement and maintain a legacy-focused mindset.

Recommended Resources:

To further your leadership development, consider these essential reads:

1. *The 21 Irrefutable Laws of Leadership* by John C. Maxwell
2. *Extreme Ownership* by Jocko Willink and Leif Babin
3. *The Difference Maker* by John C. Maxwell
4. *Make It Count* by Hunter Ballew
5. *The Great CEO Within* by Matt Mochary
6. *A CEO Only Does Three Things* by Trey Taylor

CHAPTER 2

Laying the Foundation

As a business owner looking to scale from six or seven figures up to eight figures, you might be tempted to focus solely on revenue-generating activities, but if you don't have a rock-solid foundation, you're building a house of cards that'll come tumbling down at the first sign of trouble. If your business is on a shaky foundation, then it's not going to be the type of business that a buyer is going to want to acquire. So, at this stop on the roadmap, we're going to dig into the critical elements that form the bedrock of a sustainable, scalable business.

Core Values: The Backbone of Your Business

We talked a bit about core values in your personal life and how that bleeds into the business in the previous chapter. Now, let's talk about how to create the core values that are specific to your business.

I know what you're thinking, *Hunter, come on, core values are just some fancy words we slap on the wall and forget about.*

But if that's your attitude, you're missing out on one of the most powerful tools in your business arsenal.

Core values aren't just pretty words; they're the guiding principles that shape every decision in your company. They influence your culture, your hiring and firing practices, and even how you interact with clients. Think of them as your business's DNA—they should be so ingrained in your company that they're practically second nature.

When I started Cornerstone Construction, I didn't just pull our core values out of thin air. We carefully considered what truly mattered to us as a company. Over the years, we evolved from our three original core values to a more in-depth list as our leadership team grew and began to take ownership. In the end, we landed on *integrity, ownership, teamwork, respect*, and *passion*.

I want to circle back to the example I brought up in the previous chapter because when we talk about core values, it's easy to say, "We're not going to keep people on our team if they don't abide by our core values." We had a market leader who was crushing it - I'm talking $10 million a year in revenue. But they were also inconsistent with our core values. That's the kind of performance that makes you want to turn a blind eye.

Except, at some point, you have to ask yourself, "Am I going to practice what I preach? Am I going to stand by our core values, even when it hurts?"

Then again, business isn't all black and white. Losing that market didn't just mean potentially losing its profits; it also meant that the livelihoods of the other team members employed within that market could be affected.

Still, I had to make that call because here's the brutal truth: If you're not willing to make the tough calls, your core values are just pretty words on a wall. They're not worth the paint you used to write them.

So we did it. We let that leader go. Was it comfortable? Heck no. Was it the right thing to do? Absolutely.

Look at CVS Health and former CEO, Larry Merlo. In 2014, Merlo made the decision to stop selling tobacco products in all 7,600 stores nationwide. While tobacco accounted for approximately $2 billion in annual revenue for the company, it went directly against one of their core values: promoting the health of their customers. Merlo stated, "Ending the sale of cigarettes and tobacco products at CVS Pharmacy is the right thing for us to do for our customers and our company to help people on their path to better health."

In turn, CVS's reputation as a healthcare company was strengthened, they saw an increase in partnerships with healthcare providers, and it put pressure on other retailers to reconsider their tobacco policies. This is a clear example of how a leader's commitment to core values may seem financially detrimental in the short term but align with long-term strategic goals.

Because at the end of the day, your core values aren't just about making money. They're about building a company with integrity, a company that stands for something—and sometimes that means making decisions that hurt in the short term but set you up for success in the long term.

Remember: Your team is watching. They're seeing if you really mean what you say about your core values, and if you're not willing to stick to them when it's tough, why should they?

Similar to the *Embedded* exercise where you created Life Laws, your core values should be few, memorable, and actionable. I always recommend three to five values. Any more than that, and your team won't remember them. Any less, and you're probably not covering all your bases. At Revolt, our mastermind community for business owners, we've got it down to three: *integrity, leadership,* and *legacy.* Simple, powerful, and easy to remember.

Write out twenty-plus potential core values that you stand for, then narrow it down to your top three or five:

_____   _____   _____

_____   _____   _____

_____   _____   _____

_____   _____   _____

_____   _____   _____

_____   _____   _____

_____   _____   _____

Core Values

Mission Statement: Your Company's Purpose

Next up, let's talk about your mission statement. This isn't just some corporate mumbo-jumbo to impress customers, team members, and investors. Your mission statement is your company's purpose distilled into a single, powerful sentence. What gives it that power? The fact that it is short, sweet, and packed with purpose. So, when creating your mission statement, remember that it is the driving force behind every decision your company makes, and therefore, your team should be able to recite it off the top of their heads without even pausing to think.

Try to weave your core values into your mission statement. For example, at Revolt, our mission statement is, "We bring together high-integrity individuals who are focused on developing as leaders and securing a legacy they're proud of."

See what we did there? We incorporated our core values—*integrity, leadership*, and *legacy*—right into our mission.

Let's consider another example: LinkedIn's mission statement, "Connect the world's professionals to make them more productive and successful."

This statement is concise, yet comprehensive. It clearly defines LinkedIn's purpose and target audience (professionals), while also stating the intended outcome (productivity and success). It's broad enough to allow for various business initiatives, yet specific enough to guide decision-making. It's this kind of focused, action-oriented mission statement that can be a driving force behind a company's growth and success.

Common Mission: The Glue That Binds

This is where things get really exciting. Similar to the *Defined* exercise that you completed in the previous chapter, your common mission is the impact you want to make as an organization in the outside world. It's not about profit or revenue. It's about the mark you want to leave on the world—your legacy.

At Cornerstone Construction, I wanted to figure out what our common mission was going to be, so we did something a little unconventional. We took all our sales reps out to Salt Lake City, Utah, for a personal development retreat.

So there we were, grown adults sitting cross-legged in a big circle like we were back in kindergarten.

I asked everyone, "Hey, who are the groups of people we're passionate about?"

Three main themes emerged in response: veterans, homeless people, and underprivileged children. After some discussion, we collectively decided to focus on underprivileged children.

That decision led to the creation of Cornerstone Kids, which later evolved into The Revolt Foundation—a nonprofit that now operates across the country hosting free Life 101 events for underprivileged children, where we teach kids life skills they wouldn't learn otherwise. We cover practical stuff: changing a tire, using power tools, balancing a bank account, and building credit. We also address things like developing leadership skills and physical health, as well as tough topics like preventing/dealing with addiction and how to find the right crowd to surround yourself with. It's the kind of stuff that can really change the trajectory of a kid's life.

Back in 2020, when COVID shut everything down, Cornerstone Kids saw an opportunity to make a difference by funding twelve high school proms, so seniors wouldn't miss out on this milestone. I'll never forget seeing myself and my team members, suited up and ready to dance, chaperoning these proms, doing the limbo, spinning spouses around the dance floor, passing out door prizes to the kids, and seeing firsthand the impact of our company's common mission. It was a powerful moment that brought our values to life. Not only did we help thousands of kids have one last special event before graduating, but our team and community also saw through our actions that we truly do care about more than profit.

Then you have people like Blake Mycoskie and TOMS Shoes. In 2006, Mycoskie was traveling in Argentina, where he saw kids without shoes, making them vulnerable to injury and disease.

Instead of just feeling bad about it, he thought, *What if I could build a business that helps solve this problem?*

BOOM! Mycoskie didn't just start a shoe company; he created a movement, with TOMS and its "One for One" model, which gives a pair of shoes to a child in need for every pair of shoes sold. You see, he didn't just create a charity; he built a for-profit business with giving at its core. Simple, right? But incredibly powerful.

Now, here's where it gets interesting for us as business owners. Mycoskie famously said, "Giving doesn't just feel good; it's a really good business strategy." And he's not wrong. In fact, his statement is backed by data. In 2013, TOMS had given 10 million pairs of shoes since its launch in 2006, and by 2014, the company was valued at $625 million.

Remember, your common mission isn't just about feeling good. It's about creating a purpose that your team can rally behind, that can attract customers who share your values, and that can drive your business forward. That's the power of a well-crafted common mission.

Now, let's talk about how you can create your own common mission because you've got options:

1. Donate a Percentage: Maybe it's 1 percent of your revenue or 5 percent of your profit.
2. Set Amount Per Job: You could donate a fixed dollar amount from each job.
3. Customer Involvement: Add an option on your contracts for homeowners to donate additional money to your cause.

4. Partner With Existing Nonprofits: When I started, I didn't think about partnering with existing nonprofits, but I should have. Before you create your own, check out what's already out there because there might be a perfect fit waiting for you.

Vision: Charting Your Course

When we talk about vision, we're not just daydreaming here. We're mapping out our future with laser-focused precision. So, grab a pen and paper because we're about to get specific.

First up, your one-year vision. I want you to paint a vivid picture of where you'll be 365 days from now. So, ask yourself these questions:

What does your revenue look like? Is it a number that makes you a little uncomfortable? Good. It should.

What about profit? Remember, revenue is vanity; profit is sanity.

How big is your team? Don't just throw out a number—I want you to visualize your organizational chart. Who's doing what? How many people are on your sales team? Operations? Marketing?

Here's a biggie—how much are you donating? Yeah, you heard me right. We're baking generosity into your vision from day one. Because, let me tell you, success without significance is a hollow victory.

How many projects do you need to hit these numbers? Are we talking hundreds or thousands? Think about your capacity. Are we looking at ten jobs a week, or are we scaling to fifty or one hundred? What's your average job size, and how does that translate into your revenue goals? Remember, we're not just throwing darts here. These numbers need to align with your revenue targets. If you're aiming for eight figures, you better know exactly how many jobs that breaks down to.

Pro tip: Don't just focus on quantity. Think about the quality of these jobs too. Are you going after high-ticket projects? Are you specializing in a particular niche that commands premium pricing?

Consider your sales cycle. How many leads do you need to generate to land these jobs? What's your close rate? If you need 1,000 jobs and you close one in four, you better have a plan to generate 4,000 qualified leads.

The point is, get granular. Because when you know exactly what you need to hit your targets, you can start breaking it down into monthly, weekly, and daily goals. That's how you turn this vision into reality, folks.

We're not stopping at one year; we're going big. Let's project out to five years, then ten. Where are you then? Are you dominating your local market? Have you gone national? International? Are you disrupting your entire industry?

Then, for those of you with an exit strategy in mind, let's envision that too. When do you want to sell? For how much? Or maybe you're building a legacy business to pass down. What does that look like?

Do you have the questions above answered, the numbers crunched, and the years to come mapped out? Great, because remember those three to five words we identified as your core values? It's time to weave those into your mission statement.

Now, like I said earlier, this isn't just coming up with pretty words that sound good—it's creating the DNA of your company. For instance, Apple's core values are *innovation, simplicity,* and *excellence,* and their mission statement is, "To bring the best user experience to its customers through its innovative hardware, software, and services." If we break this down, we get the following:

Innovation: Ever notice how Apple's always pushing the envelope? The iPhone wasn't just a new product; it revolutionized the entire mobile industry. That's their innovation value at work.

Simplicity: Have you ever picked up an Apple product? The interface is so intuitive a toddler could use it. That's not by accident. It's their commitment to simplicity in action.

Excellence: Apple doesn't just make good products; they obsess over every detail. The satisfying click of an iPhone button, the smooth finish of a MacBook—that's excellence in every aspect.

These values seep into everything they do. Their product design? Innovative, simple, excellent. Their retail stores? Same deal. Even their packaging screams these values.

It goes deeper than that. These values shape their hiring practices, as they don't just look for skilled workers but for people who embody their values. Their customer service is built on these principles. Do you think the Genius Bar is just a help desk? No, it's a manifestation of their commitment to excellence in user experience. Then you have their marketing, where it's all about showcasing how their products embody these values. Remember those "Think Different" ads? That's their innovation value front and center. A value we can also see in their growth strategy because they don't just enter markets; they disrupt them with innovative, simple, excellent solutions. You see, the iPod didn't just compete with other MP3 players; it changed how we consume music, and Apple continues to change how we consume and enjoy our media. Why? Because people don't just buy Apple products;

they buy into the Apple ethos; they buy into Apple's core values and mission statement.

That's the power of aligning your core values with your mission statement. That's how these two aspects can work together as a guiding force, shaping every aspect of your business. That's what it looks like to have a powerful differentiator that can propel you to the top of your industry. Obviously it's up to you to take it seriously and stick to saying what you mean like Apple; and when you do, it will help you attract the right employees, the right customers, and the right opportunities as it guides you in every decision you make.

So, when you're crafting your own values and mission, think big!

Here's your action plan:

1. Decide on your core values and craft your mission statement. Refer back to the *Embedded* exercise for inspiration.
2. Illustrate and share your vision with the team. Get them excited. Let them see the big picture.
3. Review it regularly. I'm talking at least quarterly. Keep it fresh; keep it relevant.
4. Decide on your common mission and take action.
5. Write out your one-year, five-year, and ten-year visions. Be specific about revenue, profit, team size, and giving.

Remember, a vision without action is just a daydream, but a vision built on a solid foundation of core values and a clear mission is a blueprint for success.

Also, I can't stress this enough: Don't try to do this alone. If you have a partner, spouse, or leadership team, get them involved in this process. Their input and buy-in are crucial for creating a foundation that will truly support your eight-figure vision.

We've laid the foundation in this chapter: core values, mission statement, common mission, and vision. These are the building blocks of your eight-figure business. But a foundation alone doesn't make a skyscraper, does it?

That's where the next part of our roadmap comes in. We're going to dive into the nitty-gritty of structuring for success. We're talking organizational charts, systems, processes—all the unsexy but absolutely critical stuff that turns your vision into reality.

So, do your homework. Get crystal clear on your foundation. Because in the next chapter, we're going to start building on it. And you'll be in good shape when you're starting with a solid foundation.

Remember:

1. Your core values are your business's DNA, so be ready to stand by them even when it costs you.
2. Craft a *mission statement* and *common mission* that your team can rally behind and recite easily.
3. Get specific with your vision—break down big goals into actionable numbers and steps.
4. Align your values, mission, and vision to shape every aspect of your business.
5. This foundation is crucial, but it's just the start, so gear up to build on it with the right structure and systems.

CHAPTER 3

Structured for Success

I t's time to roll up our sleeves and get into the meat and potatoes of building the structure of your business, and not just any structure—we're talking about a rock-solid organizational framework that'll make your business as sturdy as a concrete bunker.

Organizational Chart

Let's kick things off with the organizational chart or, as I'll call them moving forward, "org charts." Now, I hear you, "Hunter, org charts are about as exciting as watching grass grow." If this is your mindset, you've got it all wrong because your org chart isn't just a fancy diagram to impress visitors in your lobby. It's a living, breathing blueprint for architecting your dreams, which means a well-crafted org chart is the secret to looking ahead and scaling your business. So, let's talk about how to utilize an org chart to grow your business.

Step 1: Envision Your Future Company

First things first, pull out the vision that you crafted in the last chapter. We're not just daydreaming here—we're putting a detailed plan in place to make your vision a reality. When I started Cornerstone Construction, we were a small outfit. But I didn't build an org chart for a small company. I built it for the multimillion-dollar powerhouse I knew we could become. So, if you're currently running a $1 million operation but you're going for that $5 million mark, then you need to start thinking like a $5 million company right now. Meaning, you aren't just outlining the roles you have filled but also the roles you need filled to accomplish your vision of $5 million dollars.

Step 2: Map Out Your Ideal Structure

Now, let's get into the weeds. Grab a whiteboard or a large piece of paper. We're going to map out every single position you'll need to hit your target. Don't hold back—if you think you'll need it, put it on the chart.

For our hypothetical $5 million company, we might be looking at something like this:

- CEO
- Operations Manager
- Sales Manager
- Office Manager
- Five to Seven Sales Representatives
- Quality Control Specialist

Remember, this isn't about who you have now. This is about who you need to acquire to get where you're going.

Step 3: Define Roles and Responsibilities

After defining who you need on your org chart to achieve your vision, you'll need to establish what responsibilities each of them carry. Up to five per role is a healthy load. I'll give a few examples below.

CEO: the visionary leader who sets the course for the company.

- Responsibilities:
  1. Develop and communicate the company's vision and strategy.
  2. Make high-level decisions that shape the company's future.
  3. Foster innovation and drive growth initiatives.
  4. Oversee financial performance and resource allocation.
  5. Build and maintain a strong company culture.
  6. Represent the company in public and industry forums.

Operations Manager: the backbone of the business.

- Responsibilities:
  1. Oversee all day-to-day operations.
  2. Order materials and schedule jobs.
  3. Coordinate with other departments to optimize workflow.
  4. Drive operational efficiency and maintain quality standards.

Sales Manager: your revenue engine.

- Responsibilities:
  1. Develop and execute sales strategies.
  2. Manage and train the sales team.
  3. Set and track sales KPIs.

4. Collaborate with marketing efforts (often outsourced).
5. Maintain relationships with key accounts.

Office Manager: keeps the back office running smoothly.

- Responsibilities:
  1. Manage administrative tasks.
  2. Handle basic bookkeeping and payroll.
  3. Coordinate customer service efforts.
  4. Manage vendor relationships.
  5. Assist with HR functions.

Sales Representative: generates leads and closes sales.

- Responsibilities:
  1. Prospecting and lead generation.
  2. Execute and improve sales presentations and demonstrations.
  3. Relationship building with clients.
  4. Meet sales targets and quotas.
  5. Be up to date on market and product knowledge.

Quality Control Specialist: ensures products and/or services meet quality standards.

- Responsibilities:
  1. Conduct quality audits.
  2. Identify areas for process improvements.
  3. Ensure that all products comply with company standards.
  4. Provide training and guidance to staff on standards and procedures.
  5. Detecting and addressing quality issues.

As your company grows, so will your org chart. You'll have heads of finance, marketing, and so on. Until the cash flow affords those positions full-time, you should be able to outsource them to a reliable third-party service provider.

Step 4: Skill Set Identification

For each role, identify the key skills and attributes needed for success. This isn't just about technical skills—we're talking about the whole package.

For example, your ideal sales manager might need:

- Five or more years of sales leadership experience.
- Proven track record of hitting and exceeding targets.
- Strong analytical skills for market analysis.
- Excellent communication and interpersonal skills.
- Ability to thrive in a fast-paced, high-growth environment.

This step is crucial because it sets the standard for your hiring process down the line. What are the skill sets you will require for the other roles you're looking to fill?

Step 5: Current Team Assessment

Now, it's time for some honest evaluation. Look at your current team and see where they might fit in this new structure—and be brutally honest. Do they fit in with your growing organization? Or are they going to hold you back from growth?

I remember when we were scaling Cornerstone, I had team members who'd been with me from the start. But as we grew, some of them weren't a good fit anymore. It was one of the hardest things I've had to do, but I had to make some tough calls for the good of the rest of the team and the company.

Step 6: Gap Analysis

Compare your ideal org chart with your current team. Where are the gaps? Do you need to hire externally? Can you develop someone internally to fill a role? Look at the list of positions you need to fill, and prioritize them based on how much they impact your growth targets.

I want to share a few tips with you that I learned the hard way. First, when building out the org chart, never associate a name with the role. Second, do not create positions for people unless you need that position. Third, only after identifying the responsibilities of that role should you begin to play matchmaker with who may be the best fit. Finally, only put people in a position if their strengths match the responsibilities of that role. Anything outside of this is a disservice to them, your company, and your clients.

Step 7: Hiring and Development Plan

For roles you're filling internally, create development plans. What training or mentoring do they need to succeed in their new role?

When you think about hiring timelines, don't just focus on a specific date or time frame. For instance, someone with a plumbing company might say, "I'm not going to hire my next tech until the first tech is consistently doing $60,000 in business a month." A lot of times, financial timelines are a better measure than setting an actual date. Because if you were to give yourself three months, you might not be financially ready by then. Alternatively, you might be financially ready in thirty days, in which case, you can go ahead and hire. The key is to figure out what makes sense for your business. Just know it doesn't have to be strictly based on time.

Step 8: Compensation Structure

This is a step many forget, but it's crucial. For each role, define a compensation structure that aligns with industry standards and your company's financial projections. Remember, if you want top talent, you need to be prepared to pay for it. I've heard it said that you can pay 30 percent above market value for an "A player" and get five times the output of a "B player." The math makes sense to pay more for the *right* fit.

Step 9: Review and Adjust

Your org chart isn't set in stone. Set up quarterly reviews to assess your progress and make necessary adjustments. Are you growing faster than expected? You might need to accelerate your hiring. Hit an unexpected roadblock? You might need to pivot your structure.

Remember, this org chart is more than just boxes and lines on a page. It's the blueprint for your company's future. It's the framework that will support your growth from $1 million to $5 million to $10 million and beyond. Having all of the roles and key characteristics laid out will bring clarity to your growth strategy and save you and your team from stress and confusion in the end.

Indra Nooyi, the CEO of Pepsi from 2006 to 2018, is a perfect example of this and has spoken about the importance of a clear organizational structure in driving the company's success. She aimed to break down silos within the company and improve collaboration across different departments by using a well-defined organizational chart to clarify roles and responsibilities, which in turn helped employees understand how their work contributed to Pepsi's overall goals. During her time with Pepsi, Nooyi implemented several organizational changes that streamlined operations and fostered a culture of innovation and accountability.

KPIs

Key performance indicators (KPIs) aren't just a fancy acronym. They are the vital signs of your business—the metrics that tell you if each part of your organization is healthy and pulling its weight. Every single team member needs KPIs.

KPIs very much depend on the role. After defining the role and its five key responsibilities, the next step is to create KPIs around that role. It's crucial to tailor the KPIs to reflect the unique aspects of each role. For example, for a sales rep, the KPIs might differ based on the industry, but let's say we are deciding on KPIs for a sales rep in solar; relevant KPIs would include:

- Number of Doors Knocked: Tracking how many doors the sales rep knocks gives a measure of their activity level and effort.
- Number of Conversations Had: Assess how many meaningful interactions the sales rep is having with potential customers.
- Number of Roofs Inspected: For solar sales, getting on roofs is a critical step in the sales process, so this KPI tracks their progress in that area.
- Number of Proposals Sent Out: Measures the rep's ability to move prospects through the sales funnel to the proposal stage.

- Amount of Revenue Brought In: Measures the sales rep's effectiveness in closing deals and generating income for the company.
- Number of Contracts Signed: Tracks the final step in the sales process—securing signed agreements from customers.
- Number of Credit Checks Performed: Shows how many potential customers are being vetted for financing options.

Scorecard Example:

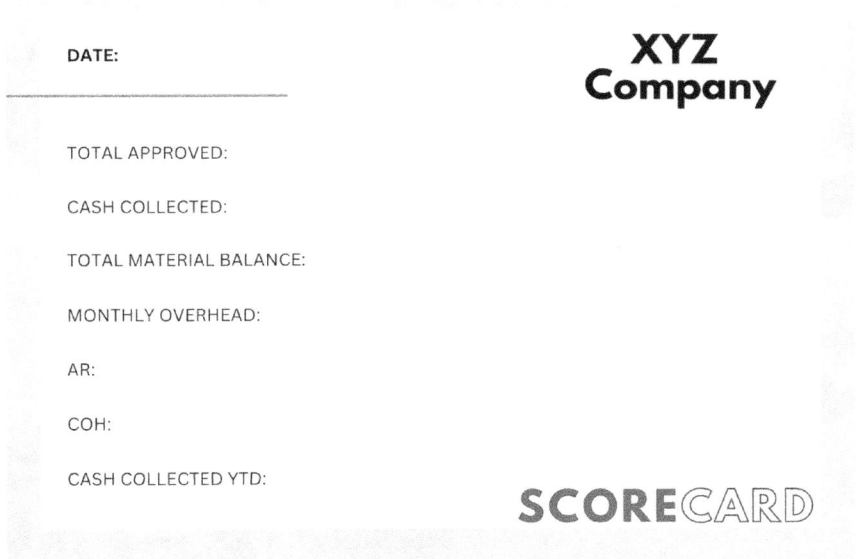

DATE:

XYZ Company

TOTAL APPROVED:

CASH COLLECTED:

TOTAL MATERIAL BALANCE:

MONTHLY OVERHEAD:

AR:

COH:

CASH COLLECTED YTD:

SCORECARD

It's important to have a manageable number of KPIs, three to five, and never exceed seven. This ensures that the KPIs remain focused and actionable without overwhelming team members.

In the roofing space, here are several key metrics to track the performance of sales reps:

- Number of Roofs Inspected: Sales reps should be getting on at least ten roofs a week, which translates to ten opportunities for potential sales.
- Revenue Generated: Tracking the amount of revenue each sales rep brings in helps us understand their impact on the company's financial health.
- Cash Collected: Focuses on the actual cash flow generated from the sales activities.
- Pipeline Approvals: Measures how many projects move through the pipeline to approval status, which provides insight into the efficiency of the sales process.
- Contracts Signed: Tracks the final agreements secured by the sales rep.
- Number of Doors Knocked: Measures the activity level of the sales reps.

For businesses outside of construction, like our mastermind, Revolt, we track different KPIs. These effectively measure our performance, identify areas for improvement, and drive our business toward its goals in accordance with our unique business model:

- Number of New Members Signed up Each Month: Measures our growth and ability to attract new members.
- Number of Old Members Renewed Each Month: Tracks renewals to understand member satisfaction and loyalty because retaining existing members is crucial.
- Cash Collected: Just like in sales, tracking cash flow is essential for financial health.
- Overhead Costs: Helps us manage expenses and maintain profitability.
- Monthly Churn Rate for Old Members: Tracks how many members leave each month, providing insight into member retention and satisfaction.

Here's how we structure our KPIs:

1. The Minimum Threshold: The "you better hit this or we've got problems" number.
2. The Target: Hit this consistently, and you're doing your job well.
3. The Stretch: Hit this, and it's reward time.

Now, we don't just set these KPIs and forget about them. We're tracking these numbers every single week on a scorecard, and then we review them in weekly one-on-one meetings. That's right, every week. Beyond that, we monitor a monthly tracker to see month-over-month (MoM) activity.

It's essential to tailor your KPIs to your unique business model and objectives, so you have to think about what makes sense for your company and the specific roles within it. Only then can you come up with your own KPIs.

Monthly KPI Tracker in Google Sheets

KPI	Goal	Minimum	Example	Janurary	February
Leads	160	80	92		
CAC	< $325	< $750	$250		
Overhead	< $50,000	< $70,000	$40,000		
AR	<$100,000	<$200,000	$240,000		
Cash Collected	$250,000	$150,000	$340,000		
COH	$500,000	$250,000	$212,000		
Reviews	> 10	> 5	12		

On Goal	
On Minimum	
Off Target	

One Month	Warning
Two Months	Probation
Three Months	20% Salary Reduction
Four Months	Termination

This applies to missing minimums*

Meetings

Ask anyone and they'll tell you I'm not a big meetings guy. But meetings are a necessary evil in business. As the business owner, I set the tone. I set the culture. So even if meetings aren't my jam, I show up and I set the example. That means having a positive attitude, getting everyone fired up about good news, and then rolling up my sleeves to dive into those KPIs and problem-solving to overcome any obstacles.

That being said, if I'm going to have a meeting, then I want to make sure it counts. Don't just have meetings for the sake of having meetings. If you're sixteen minutes into a ninety-minute meeting and you're twiddling your thumbs, then it's time to wrap it up. Meeting just to meet is a waste of the company's resources and everyone's time.

I want to show you how we kick off each week.

Monday: Housekeeping

Every Monday is dedicated to internal meetings only. No external appointments. Why? Because alignment starts at home. We need to get our house in order before we deal with the outside world.

Monday Mornings: Leadership Meeting

We kick off every week with a leadership meeting. Here's how we structure it:

1. Good News: We start with the positives. It sets the tone for the meeting and reminds us why we're doing this in the first place.
2. KPI Review: We dive into the numbers. Where are we crushing it? Where are we falling short?

3. Problem-Solving: We're not just identifying problems—we're solving them. At times, we even invite people from different parts of the company to these meetings. Why? Because sometimes the best solutions come from unexpected places. You never know. Your marketing guru might have the perfect insight into an operations issue.

4. Focus Points: We identify tasks and projects that we need to knock out and put in our project management software.

Monday Afternoons: One-on-One Meetings

After our leadership meeting, it's time for one-on-one meetings with direct reports. For me, I'm meeting with the presidents of each of my companies, and they're cascading down to their direct reports with one-on-ones after that.

In these one-on-ones, we're reviewing their KPI scorecards, we're problem-solving, and we're strategizing. It's not just about the numbers—it's about growth, both for the individual and the company.

Tuesday: Company-wide Meeting

The outline of this meeting is very similar to Monday's leadership meeting. Again, we're seeking perspective from people within the organization that may have an idea and be able to provide some better insight than we're having because they have a different vantage point. There's also some transparency, where we talk about where the numbers are. If we're not doing so hot, we'll problem-solve together.

As I always say, "I don't care whose idea it is. All I care about is that it's the best idea to help our company achieve the goals that we have."

We do our sales team meetings on Tuesday, as well. We review KPIs, problem-solving, and getting creative as a company. We also add in training, role-play, and more specific sales activities.

Monthly Feedback Loop

Once a month, we hold a feedback session. We're talking about a monthly one-on-one, no-holds-barred, growth-focused conversation with your direct reports. Our model is simple:

"I like that you're doing ABC. I wish that you would do XYZ."

But don't let the simplicity fool you. This structure is powerful. It acknowledges the good while pushing for better, and here's the kicker—after I dish it out, I've got to take it. That's right, they give me feedback too. Give room for them to get things off their chest and provide feedback about you as the leader.

Now, why do we do this dance at least once a month? Because it keeps the nasty stuff from festering. You know what I'm talking about—those little annoyances that build up over time until you're ready to explode. We're nipping that in the bud.

Think about it. If you're only having these conversations once or twice a year, you're letting six months of frustration build up. That's a recipe for disaster. When you're tackling issues head-on every month, you're constantly clearing the air.

So, pro tip: Schedule these feedback sessions. It's right there on the calendar, with a note saying, "It's your responsibility to initiate the feedback session." No surprises, no ambushes. Everyone knows it's coming, and everyone's prepared.

This isn't about catching people off guard or playing "gotcha." It's about creating a culture of continuous improvement.

Project Management Tools

When I use the term "project management," I don't mean the kind where you're managing a homeowner's project or a commercial project like in the contracting space. I'm referring to managing projects within your business. This is where tools like Asana, Trello, and Monday.com come into play.

We personally use Monday.com to keep track of our focus points, everything we need to work on to take our business to the next level. Anything that needs attention goes inside Monday.com, and it's assigned to the person in our organization responsible for handling it.

So, let's say we need to build out our recruiting funnel. First, I go into Monday.com and create a new task called, "Recruiting Funnel." Next, I set a deadline for this task. Deadlines are crucial because they give a clear timeframe for when the task needs to be completed by. Without a deadline, they get looked at but never prioritized, dragging on indefinitely.

Once I set the deadline, I assign an owner to the task. It's extremely important to have one person accountable for getting the task done. This is what we mean by having "one throat to choke." This single point of accountability ensures that there's no confusion about who's responsible for completing the task and takes the emotion out of the conversation during your weekly and monthly meetings.

Next, I'll assign team members to assist the task owner through a customized field named, "Team." If I don't know who the team members will be, I let the task owner pick their own team. This allows for flexibility and ensures that the task owner can choose people who are best suited to help complete the task.

When the owner gets alerted about the new task, they need to change the status from "new" to "accepted." This signifies that they've acknowledged the task and are taking responsibility for it. As they start working on it, they'll change the status to "in progress." Once the task is complete, they'll mark it as "completed." Having these different stages allows the leadership team to see how often this specific task is being worked on and how efficiently the team is working to get it to the completed stage.

Every single day, team members log in to Monday.com, check their list of tasks, organize them by deadline, and make sure they're completing their focus points. This daily routine ensures that nothing falls through the cracks and that we're constantly moving the company forward.

Automations within Monday.com can streamline the process even further. For example, you can set up an automation to move the task through different stages of completion, and then send a task to the review section for leadership. Once it's reviewed and approved by leadership, it will be archived.

Finally, the last project management tip I'll give is to have someone in charge of reviewing each task and the deadline at least weekly, if not daily. Have this person tag the owner in the notes section to give them a nudge and ask where they're at or if they need help. It's a small task but can make a big difference in productivity, and it is a position that can even be filled by a virtual assistant.

Access An Explainer Of Our Monday.com Setup Here: TheRevolt. com/roadmap

Having all of our projects within the business tracked in a project management software like Monday.com is a game-changer. Instead of relying on sticky notes, whiteboards, or pieces of paper that can easily get lost or forgotten, it creates a structured environment where everyone knows their responsibilities, deadlines are clear, and progress is transparent. This allows us to ensure that our business runs smoothly and efficiently, allowing us to focus on growth and success.

Calendar Management

Another key element to being structured for success is calendar management. Effective calendar management goes beyond just scheduling meetings; it's about creating a visual representation of your priorities and making sure you're dedicating the right amount of time to each area of your life and business. This way, you ensure that you're not only productive but also balanced, making time for both professional responsibilities and personal commitments.

One powerful tool in calendar management is color coding. Using a tool like Google Calendar, you can color code your events, which will allow you to get a clear visual of where you're spending your time when you pair it with "Time Insights"—a feature inside Google Calendar.

For example, as I mentioned earlier, Mondays are dedicated to internal meetings, so we color code these as gray. For external meetings, such as calls with members of our mastermind group, sales calls, podcasts, or other external interactions, I use different colors. Here's how it breaks down:

- Internal Meetings: gray
- External Meetings: yellow
- Chief Problem-Solver: orange
- Money Meetings: dark green
- Podcasts: light green
- Off-Site Meetings: purple
- Travel: pink
- Urgent: red

Time breakdown ⓘ ✏

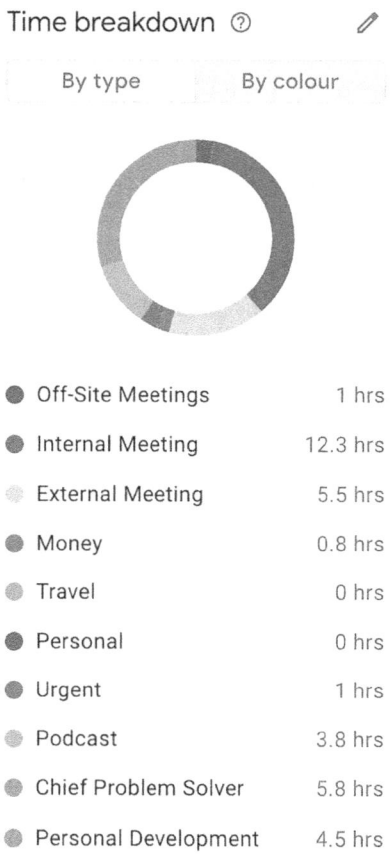

⬤ Off-Site Meetings	1 hrs
⬤ Internal Meeting	12.3 hrs
⬤ External Meeting	5.5 hrs
⬤ Money	0.8 hrs
⬤ Travel	0 hrs
⬤ Personal	0 hrs
⬤ Urgent	1 hrs
⬤ Podcast	3.8 hrs
⬤ Chief Problem Solver	5.8 hrs
⬤ Personal Development	4.5 hrs

The reason this system works so well is that your brain starts to associate each color with a specific type of task or meeting, helping you stay organized and prepared. For example, I mark off-site meetings in purple. Seeing that purple on my calendar signals that I need to be ready more than five minutes before the meeting time because I have to get up and go somewhere. So as you can see, by using this color-coded system, I can evaluate what my day looks like at a glance, ensuring I'm making the best use of my time. For urgent and important personal events, like my son's soccer game, I use red. This color signifies the importance and urgency, making sure it catches my eye whenever I glance at my calendar so I don't forget it.

Leadership Team Development

Continuing to develop your leadership team is crucial, as your efforts trickle down to your other team members, eventually affecting your entire company. This development can take many forms. Hosting company retreats provides a fantastic opportunity for team bonding and skill-building outside the usual work environment. Bringing in external experts or coaches can provide fresh perspectives and specialized training that can be incredibly valuable. Providing them with resources like books to read is another great way to foster continuous learning and development.

Books I recommend:

- *Atomic Habits* by James Clear
- *Drive: The Surprising Truth About What Motivates Us* by Daniel H. Pink
- *The 7 Habits of Highly Effective People* by Stephen R. Covey
- *Good to Great: Why Some Companies Make the Leap . . . and Others Don't* by Jim Collins

It's not just about the immediate benefits but about creating a culture of growth and improvement. Regularly investing in your team's development ensures they are constantly evolving, which, in turn, propels your business forward. This ongoing development is paramount to sustaining long-term success and maintaining a motivated, high-performing team.

Thinking Ahead

One point I want to emphasize is a quote you've probably heard, "If you fail to plan, you plan to fail."

Think about that for a moment.

It's a simple, but powerful reminder of the importance of foresight and preparation. Without a plan, you're essentially setting yourself up for failure.

Having a vision is just the beginning. When you create your vision for where you want your business to go, you need to ensure you have the right pieces in place. To turn that vision into reality, you need to meticulously plan each step, ensuring every aspect of your business is aligned with your long-term goals. This involves everything from setting clear targets and milestones to establishing the necessary infrastructure and resources. This means developing the right systems and processes that support your goals and creating a detailed roadmap that guides you toward your objectives.

In essence, planning is about setting yourself up for success. It's about structuring your business in a way that not only meets immediate needs but also anticipates future challenges and opportunities. By doing so, you create a solid foundation that enables sustainable growth and resilience in the face of uncertainty.

Remember, success doesn't happen by accident. It's the result of deliberate planning and strategic action. So, take the time to plan thoroughly and thoughtfully. Your future self—and your business—will thank you for it.

In Chapter 4 of this roadmap, we'll explore the fundamentals of your finances so you can operate your business at the highest level.

Remember:

1. Your org chart is the blueprint for your domain—design it for where you're going, not where you are, and be ready to make tough calls on who fits where.
2. KPIs are your business's vital signs—track three to five per role weekly, tailor them to each position, and use them to drive performance.
3. Structure your meetings for maximum impact—start with good news, review KPIs, problem-solve, and set clear focus points.
4. Implement a monthly feedback loop with your team—"I like that you're doing ABC. I wish that you would do XYZ." Allow space for your team to do the same. It keeps the air clear and drives continuous improvement.
5. Use project management tools religiously—assign owners, set deadlines, and track progress daily to keep your business moving forward.
6. Color code your calendar to optimize your time—visually organize your commitments, and audit where you're spending your energy.

CHAPTER 4

Financial Fundamentals

This stop on the roadmap is where we get real about what makes or breaks a business—knowing your numbers. When you're growing a company, your first instinct is to focus on making sales rather than balancing books. But here's the truth: You can't scale to eight figures *and sustain it* if you don't understand your financials inside and out.

I know some of you might be thinking, *I didn't become an entrepreneur to go cross-eyed over spreadsheets all day.* Trust me, I get it. It's my least favorite part of the job too, but in this chapter, we're going to clarify those financial statements that might look like a foreign language to some of you. By the time we're done, you'll have a clear understanding of how profit and loss statements, cash flow statements, and balance sheets affect your business.

First, we'll go through profit and loss statements, then cash flow statements. Because, I want it to be very clear – revenue isn't cash, and profit isn't cash either. I've seen too many businesses struggle because they didn't understand this difference. You'll learn why a profitable business can still run into trouble, and how to make sure that doesn't happen to you.

Then we'll touch on balance sheets. This is where you'll get a snapshot of your business's financial health at any given moment. We'll cover assets, liabilities, and equity. You'll learn how to use your balance sheet to make smart decisions about investments, loans, and growth strategies.

And here's something that trips up even experienced business owners: understanding the key financial terms. We're going to clear up the difference between revenue, gross profit, and net profit. No more confusion, no more guesswork.

By the end of this chapter, you'll be able to look at your financial statements and see the story they're telling about your business. You'll be able to make decisions based on facts, not just instinct. And when you're operating at eight figures, you need more than just gut feelings.

I know this might feel overwhelming just thinking about all this financial talk. But here's the thing—this isn't about turning you into an accountant. It's about giving you the tools you need to be an effective business owner. Because when you understand your numbers, you're not just running a business—you're controlling its future.

Profit and Loss Statements (P&Ls)

First up, profit and loss statements. This isn't just a fancy name for how much money you made last month. We're going to break down every line item, from revenue to cost of goods sold to operating expenses. You'll learn how to read these month over month and year over year, easily spotting trends, identifying problem areas, and finding opportunities for growth that you might be missing.

So, let's break down the financial fundamentals of your business, and focus on the key components of your profit and loss statement by digging into what each element means, and why it matters for your eight-figure journey.

1. **Revenue**

    o   This is the total amount of money coming into your business.

    o   It's the top line of your profit and loss statement.

    o   Example: If you complete a $10,000 job, your revenue is $10,000.

Understanding revenue is crucial, but it's just the starting point. Don't make the rookie mistake of thinking all that money is yours to keep. Let's dig deeper.

2. **Cost of Goods Sold (COGS)**

    o   This is what it costs you to complete a job or deliver your service.

    o   Includes things like:

        ▪   Labor costs
        ▪   Subcontractor fees
        ▪   Material costs
        ▪   Sales commissions

    o   Example: If your COGS on that $10,000 job is $5,000 or 50 percent of revenue, let's say $2,000 in subcontractor fees, $1,000 in commission and $2,000 in material, that includes all the costs directly associated with completing the job.

Here's where many business owners start to get a reality check. That $10,000 job? Half of it is already spoken for just to cover the basic costs of doing the work.

3. Gross Profit

- o This is what's left after you subtract COGS from revenue.
- o It's a critical number because it shows how much money you have to cover overhead and (hopefully) generate a profit.
- o Keep in mind that you may have heard of "gross margin." That's just your gross profit described in a percentage. So in this case, the gross margin would be 50 percent.
- o Example: On our $10,000 job with $5,000 COGS, the gross profit is $5,000 (50 percent of revenue).

Now, don't get excited and think this $5,000 is net profit. We're not done yet. This is where many business owners get tripped up, thinking they have more money to play with than they actually do.

4. Overhead

- o Some say overhead and some say operating expenses.
- o We will keep it simple. These are the costs of running your business that aren't directly tied to producing your product or service.
- o Includes things like:
  - Salaries
  - Rent
  - Utilities
  - Vehicle expenses
  - Insurance
- o Some overhead is fixed (like rent or salaries); some is variable (like utilities).
- o Example: Let's say your monthly overhead typically runs about 30 percent of revenue. On our $10,000 job, that's $3,000.

This is where reality really sets in for many business owners. You thought you had $5,000 left after COGS, but now another $3,000 is gone just to keep the lights on.

5. Net Profit

- o This is what's left after you subtract both COGS and overhead from revenue.
- o It's the bottom line—literally and figuratively.
- o Example: On our $10,000 job, with $5,000 COGS and $3,000 overhead, the net profit is $2,000 (20 percent of revenue).

This is the real measure of how your business is performing. It's what you have left to reinvest in the business, pay yourself, or save for a rainy day.

Now, here's the kicker—you typically wouldn't calculate this on a job-by-job basis. Instead, you'd look at these numbers over the course of a month. Why? Because while your COGS might be pretty consistent per job, your overhead doesn't neatly divide up by job. Some months you might do more jobs but have the same overhead, meaning each job is more profitable.

Understanding these components—revenue, COGS, gross profit, overhead, and net profit—is absolutely crucial to running a successful business. If you don't know these numbers, you're flying blind, and in the world of eight-figure businesses, blind pilots don't last long.

Remember, just because you see money coming in doesn't mean it's all profit. Too many business owners see their gross profit and think that's what they have to spend. That's a one-way ticket to financial trouble.

By really grasping these concepts, you'll be able to make informed decisions about pricing, cost control, and growth strategies. You'll know exactly how much wiggle room you have and where you can optimize. This isn't just about understanding numbers—it's about using those numbers to drive your business forward.

Below you'll find an example of a profit and loss statement. Feel free to take this example and apply it to your own business.

XYZ Contracting Services
Profit and Loss Statement
For the month ending December 31, 2023

Revenue:	$100,000
Cost of Goods Sold:	
Labor	$30,000
Materials	$15,000
Subcontractor Fees	$10,000
Sales Commissions	$5,000
Total Cost of Goods Sold:	($60,000)
Gross Profit:	$40,000
Operating Expenses:	
Salaries and Wages	$15,000
Rent	$3,000
Utilities	$1,000
Vehicle Expenses	$2,000
Insurance	$1,500
Marketing	$2,500
Office Supplies	$500
Miscellaneous	$1,500
Total Operating Expenses:	($27,000)
Net Profit:	$13,000
Gross Profit Margin: 40%	
Net Profit Margin: 13%	

Cash Flow Statements

A cash flow statement is a financial document that shows how cash is moving in and out of your business during a specific time period. It's like a detailed bank statement for your company but with more insight into where the money's coming from and going to.

Here's why it's important: You can be profitable on paper but still run out of cash because profit doesn't always equal cash in the bank. A cash flow statement helps you understand if you've got enough cash to keep the lights on and the business running.

The cash flow statement is typically divided into three main sections:

1. Cash from Operating Activities: This is the cash generated from your core business operations. It includes cash received from customers and cash paid out for things like supplies, wages, and taxes.
2. Cash from Investing Activities: This shows cash used for or generated from investments. It might include purchases of equipment or property, or cash received from selling assets.
3. Cash from Financing Activities: This section covers cash related to funding your business. It includes things like taking out or repaying loans, or issuing and buying back shares if you're a corporation.

The bottom line of your cash flow statement shows the net increase or decrease in cash for the period. This number is crucial because it tells you if you're building up cash reserves or if you're burning through cash.

Now, here's why understanding your cash flow statement is vital for scaling to eight figures:

1. It helps you predict future cash needs. If you're planning to expand, you need to know if you'll have the cash to do it.
2. It shows you where your cash is coming from. Are you relying too heavily on loans? Or is your core business generating plenty of cash?
3. It helps you spot trends. Maybe you're consistently cash-poor in certain months. Knowing this can help you plan better.
4. It can reveal problems that aren't obvious on your P&L. You might be profitable, but if all your cash is tied up in inventory or unpaid invoices, you could still be in trouble.

Remember, cash is king. You can't pay your bills with profit—you need actual cash. That's why understanding your cash flow statement is just as important as knowing your P&L and balance sheet.

Below is an example of a cash flow statement:

XYZ Contracting Services
Cash Flow Statement
For the month ending December 31, 2023

Cash Flow from Operating Activities:	
Net Income	$13,000
Adjustments for non-cash items:	
Depreciation	$2,000
Changes in working capital:	
Increase in Accounts Receivable	($15,000)
Decrease in Inventory	$5,000
Increase in Accounts Payable	$8,000
Increase in Accrued Expenses	$3,000
Net Cash from Operating Activities	$16,000
Cash Flow from Investing Activities:	
Purchase of Equipment	($10,000)
Net Cash used in Investing Activities	($10,000)
Cash Flow from Financing Activities:	
Repayment of Short-Term Loan	($5,000)
Net Cash used in Financing Activities	($5,000)
Net Increase in Cash	$1,000
Cash at Beginning of Period	$49,000
Cash at End of Period	$50,000

This cash flow statement shows that despite earning a net income of $13,000, XYZ Contracting's actual increase in cash was only $1,000. Here's why:

1. Operating Activities: While the company made a profit, a significant amount ($15,000) is tied up in accounts receivable—money earned but not yet received. This is partially offset by positive changes in inventory and payables.
2. Investing Activities: The company invested $10,000 in new equipment, using up cash.
3. Financing Activities: They paid down $5,000 of a short-term loan.

This statement reveals that while XYZ Contracting is profitable, they need to keep an eye on their cash management. The increase in accounts receivable suggests they might need to improve their collection processes, turning those sales into cash faster.

This cash flow statement ties directly to the balance sheet. In other words, the ending cash balance of $50,000 matches the "Cash and Cash Equivalents" line on the balance sheet in the next section.

Balance Sheets

It's called a balance sheet because it's based on the fundamental accounting equation: Liabilities + Owner's Equity = Assets, which in turn provides you a snapshot of your financial position at a single point in time. This snapshot—what your company owns (assets), owes (liabilities), and the owner's equity—always needs to balance. Think of it as a financial health checkup.

Now, the next thing you need to understand is how a balance sheet works with a P&L. While the P&L focuses on operational performance, the balance sheet indicates your company's overall financial stability and potential for growth. Therefore, the P&L helps with day-to-day operational decisions, the balance sheet aids in longer term financial planning, and together they give you a comprehensive view of your business's financial situation, which is critical as you scale toward eight figures.

With the basics addressed, let's dive a bit deeper with a breakdown of the main components:

1. Assets: These are resources owned by the company that have economic value. Assets are typically listed in order of liquidity (how quickly they can be converted to cash).
   o Current Assets: These can be converted to cash within one year.
      ▪ Cash and Cash Equivalents
      ▪ Accounts Receivable
      ▪ Inventory
      ▪ Prepaid Expenses
   o Fixed Assets: These are long-term assets not easily converted to cash.
      ▪ Property, Plant, and Equipment
      ▪ Vehicles
      ▪ Furniture and Fixtures
   o Intangible Assets:
      ▪ Goodwill
      ▪ Patents
      ▪ Trademarks
2. Liabilities: These are the company's financial obligations or debts.
   o Current Liabilities: debts due within one year.
      ▪ Accounts Payable
      ▪ Short-Term Loans

- Current Portion of Long-Term Debt
- Accrued Expenses
  - o Long-Term Liabilities: debts due after one year.
    - Long-Term Loans
    - Bonds Payable
    - Deferred Tax Liabilities
3. Owner's Equity: This represents the owner's investment in the business plus retained earnings.
   - o Capital Stock (for corporations)
   - o Retained Earnings
   - o Additional Paid-In Capital

The balance sheet is important because it shows:

1. Liquidity: How easily can your business meet its short-term obligations?
2. Leverage: How much of your business is financed by debt versus equity?
3. Efficiency: How effectively are you using your assets to generate revenue?
4. Overall Financial Health: Are your assets greater than your liabilities?

Understanding your balance sheet is crucial for making informed decisions about your business. It can help you determine if you can afford to take on more debt, if you need to collect receivables more quickly, or if you're in a position to expand.

Remember, a strong balance sheet typically shows more assets than liabilities and a healthy amount of owner's equity. What's considered "good" can vary by industry, so it's important to compare your balance sheet to industry standards and your own historical performance.

Here is an example of a balance sheet:

XYZ Contracting Services
Balance Sheet
As of December 31, 2023

ASSETS
Current Assets:

Cash and Cash Equivalents	$50,000
Accounts Receivable	$75,000
Inventory	$30,000
Prepaid Expenses	$5,000
Total Current Assets	$160,000

Fixed Assets:

Vehicles	$80,000
Equipment	$70,000
Less: Accumulated Depreciation	($30,000)
Total Fixed Assets	$120,000

TOTAL ASSETS	$280,000

LIABILITIES
Current Liabilities:

Accounts Payable	$40,000
Short-Term Loans	$20,000
Accrued Expenses	$15,000
Total Current Liabilities	$75,000

Long-Term Liabilities:	
Long-Term Loans	$60,000
Total Long-Term Liabilities	$60,000
TOTAL LIABILITIES	$135,000
OWNER'S EQUITY	
Owner's Capital	$100,000
Retained Earnings	$45,000
Total Owner's Equity	$145,000
TOTAL LIABILITIES AND OWNER'S EQUITY	$280,000

This snapshot shows XYZ Contracting has a solid asset base, manageable debt levels, and a healthy amount of owner's equity, indicating good financial health and potential for further growth. How do we know this? The sum of liabilities and owner's equity equals the total assets, which maintains the fundamental accounting equation: Liabilities + Owner's Equity = Assets.

What if the balance sheet doesn't balance? At some point, you will experience financial challenges, and having been through the wringer with this, I want to share some hard-earned wisdom with you on understanding your numbers.

First things first: Look at your numbers every single day. I can't stress this enough. It may sound daunting, but make it a habit to at least do a quick daily review of the cash on hand. As you build a team with a CFO, controller, or office manager—you can have them send you a report each morning with Cash On Hand, while every week you are reviewing your scorecard with Cash On Hand, AR, AP, etc. It might seem tedious, but trust me, it'll help you make better decisions in the long run and eliminate the chance of you ignoring finances because you don't like to look.

When we first hit eight figures in annual revenue at Cornerstone, we were on cloud nine. We were selling over a million dollars a month, and I remember one day we closed over a hundred contracts totaling a million dollars in a single day. Sounds impressive, right?

Well, here's the truth—we were selling these jobs without a sustainable profit margin. We didn't have the right checks and balances in place to ensure profitability. When we finally took a hard look at our numbers, we realized our gross profit was only 28 percent, with overhead eating up 25 percent. That left us with just 3 percent net profit.

Now, 3 percent might not sound bad, but it's not enough to sustain and grow a business. It took bringing in people smarter than me to figure out we had to stop the, "We'll sell it, we'll build it, we'll figure it out on the back end," mentality. That approach just doesn't work in the long run. Instead, we needed to be smarter about how we operated and make sure we were left in a good spot after every job. This meant being closer to a 40 percent gross profit, with overhead at 20 to 25 percent, leaving us with a healthy 15 to 20 percent net profit. The lesson: Sell less product at a higher margin if it means acquiring the same net profit as you would selling more product at a lower margin. Why? Less liability, less headache—the list goes on.

Another crucial lesson I've seen many fail to learn until it's too late—the difference between margin and markup, because it can make or break your profitability. So, let me break it down for you:

Let's say your cost to do a job is $10,000. If you mark it up 50 percent, you're selling the job at $15,000, leaving you with $5,000 profit. Reality check—that $5,000 is actually only a 33 percent profit margin because it's based on the total job price of $15,000. Therefore, if you wanted a true 50 percent profit margin, you'd need to sell that same job for $20,000. Your cost is still $10,000, but now you're left with a $10,000 profit—that's your 50 percent margin. Notice this is actually a 100 percent markup on your costs.

You need to look at your numbers before committing to any job. Put protections in place so you don't end up in a tight spot. It's not enough to just sell a lot—you need to sell smart. Remember, in this game, it's not about how much you make; it's about how much you keep. Don't let impressive sales numbers blind you to the reality of your profit margins.

Job Profitability

Now that you know your numbers, let's talk about making them into a powerhouse for your business. I'm going to share a resource that I built years ago that simplifies finance—a Job Profitability Sheet. It's a Google Sheet I've been using since the beginning and has continued to evolve to track every single job and every single number.

Now, I know what you're thinking, *Hunter, don't you have a CRM and QuickBooks?* Of course we do, but there's something about getting your hands dirty with the numbers in a spreadsheet that gives you insights you can't get anywhere else. For me, it provides better visibility.

Access The Job Profitability Sheet Here: TheRevolt.com/roadmap

This sheet is our financial bible. We can see the revenue for each job, the total for the month, the margin on each job, cost of goods sold, labor, materials, sales commission—you name it. We can even spot trends month to month. Are we suddenly paying 2 percent more in labor? Has our material cost spiked? These red flags can save you if you catch them early.

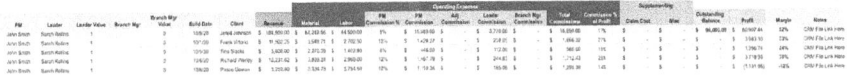

On a $10 million business, a 1 percent difference is $100,000. That's not a small number. It's the difference in team bonuses, the trip you wanted to take your spouse on, and so many other things. It's why negotiation matters so dang much. You've got to negotiate hard on everything: labor, sales commissions, supplier pricing. And don't forget about those rebates. In some cases, those rebates are tax-free, so it's like finding money in your couch cushions, but way better. Depending on your industry, you'll have trips, gift cards, and apparel thrown at you from manufacturers and suppliers. What if you put more emphasis on the pricing of the product you are getting? We've had an owner come to our two-day training, and then go home and use our "Performance-Based" scripts to negotiate pricing and make an additional $117,000 in a single year just through getting better rates. We always strive to make it a win-win for both parties.

Overhead

You've got to be ruthless here. Know your customer acquisition cost (CAC), your lead costs, all the levers you can pull to grow profitably, and whatever you do, keep an eye on your expenses. If you've got a sales rep on salary who's not pulling their weight, you've got to cut them loose. Same goes for marketing campaigns or agencies that aren't delivering a return on investment (ROI). They're like leeches, sucking you dry if you let them – even if that's not their intention. It's not personal; it's business.

Warren Buffett invested in a textile company called Berkshire Hathaway back in the day. Every week, he'd pore over their production and inventory figures. One week, he noticed that one of the inventory categories was piling up. He called the president and asked about it. Turns out, they were about to close a plant but hadn't announced it yet. Buffett's attention to detail gave him insider knowledge that helped him make better investment decisions. The lesson? Know your numbers, folks. They tell a story if you're willing to listen.

Turn Expenses Into Profit Centers

This leads us into my next piece of advice—the concept of turning the expenses worth keeping into profit centers. This is a game-changer, and it ties directly into what I've been talking about with understanding your finances and maximizing profitability. This is part two of looking at your numbers daily and understanding your margins.

It's not just about cutting costs or raising prices—it's about getting creative with your existing resources. Here are a couple of examples of this in my own businesses.

In the contracting world, we use something called a Catch-All. It's a protective measure that keeps debris from damaging the homeowner's property during a project. Now, typically, this is seen as an expense—you've got to buy the equipment, and sometimes pay your crew extra to set it up. But here's where the mindset shift comes into play. What if, instead of treating it as a cost, you offer it as a premium service? Charge extra for it. Suddenly, that expense becomes a profit center to increase your margin! I've seen it done many times.

In our mastermind program, Revolt, we have a full-time videographer on staff. On paper, their salary is an expense. Here's how we turned that expense into a profit center: we started offering video services to our Revolt members. Here's how it shows up in the financials. Say you're paying your videographer $50,000 a year. That's a significant expense. But what if you could find twelve companies willing to pay $5,000 each for video work? That equates to $60,000 generated from what was previously just a cost.

Now, you might be thinking, *Hunter, that's only $10,000 profit.*

That's not the point.

The point is you've completely erased that salary expense, and if you want to get really creative, split that extra $10,000 with your videographer. Now, they're motivated to bring in more business, and you've turned a $50,000 expense into a break-even proposition with potential for growth. In our model at Revolt, this makes a lot of sense, as we already work with other business owners. In some business models you'd only be creating a distraction. You have to take a hard look at your model and expenses to see what makes sense.

The key is to stop seeing your resources as just costs. Look at every expense and ask yourself, "Can I turn this into a revenue stream?" Maybe it's offering premium services, maybe it's leveraging your team's skills for additional income, or maybe it's finding new uses for equipment that sits idle part of the time. This ties directly back to what we've been discussing about understanding your finances. When you're looking at your numbers daily and understanding your finances, you're not just tracking expenses—you're identifying opportunities. Every line item in your expenses could be a potential goldmine if you approach it with the right mindset.

So, I challenge you: Take a hard look at your expense sheet. Pick one item and brainstorm ways to turn it into a profit center. It might feel uncomfortable at first, but that's where the magic happens. That's how you start to separate yourself from the pack and build a truly profitable, scalable business. It's not just about working harder – it's about working smarter.

Forecasting

All right, let's talk forecasting—the crystal ball of business. Hard numbers and smart planning. Finding a third party to help you forecast can be a real game-changer. Why? They bring an objective perspective to the table. They're not emotionally tied to your business. Plus, an experienced CPA or bookkeeper has likely seen more than you. They can spot trends and potential issues that you might miss while you're busy running the show. And let's face it, you've got a business to run. Outsourcing this task frees you up to focus on what you do best.

Now, if you decide to bring someone in-house, remember this: experience matters. Don't cheap out on this hire. Look for someone who's been in the trenches, who understands your industry, and who can grow with your business. Here's the part that keeps me up at night: fraud. It happens more often than you'd think. So put protections in place. Segregate duties, perform regular audits, and use technology to your advantage. Remember, trust is good, but verification is better. Don't be afraid to put checks and balances in place with multiple sets of eyes internally and/or externally.

Profit First

Growth often comes with more extreme peaks and valleys, leading to increased financial stress. But there's a way to manage these swings.

The key? Profit first. It's a philosophy that can save your business, and here's how it works:

1. As soon as money comes in, set aside a predetermined percentage for profit.
2. Pay yourself a salary—yes, even if you're the owner.
3. Set aside money for taxes.
4. What's left is what you have to run your business.

This approach forces you to run leanly and efficiently. It's like creating your own rainy day fund, and in business, it always rains eventually.

The big idea here is to set aside your profit as soon as the money comes in. You can even set up an automation, with an app like Sequence or

Astra, so that the money is moved without you ever having to think about it. Maybe it's 5 percent, maybe it's 10 percent, but you decide and stick to it. If you don't, you'll always find a reason to "invest" that money back into the business. Next thing you know, you're robbing Peter to pay Paul, and speaking from experience, that's a slippery slope, my friends.

For more on this concept, read *Profit First* by Mike Michalowicz.

Tying it All Together

It's okay to be aggressive and push for fast growth. But if you don't manage your money well, you're setting yourself up for disaster. You might end up having to fire good people just to keep the lights on. Or worse, you might keep the wrong people because you can't afford to replace them.

The bottom line: Understanding your numbers isn't just important—it's paramount. It's the difference between a business that survives and one that thrives. If you're looking at your money daily and doing financial reviews monthly, you're going to make better decisions. Period. It's not the sexiest part of running a business, but it's the foundation everything else is built on.

Here's your homework:

1. Start tracking your numbers daily.
2. Set up your Job Profitability Sheet.
3. Implement "Profit First" in your business.
4. Get a third-party perspective on your finances.

In the world of business, knowledge truly is power, and when it comes to your finances, ignorance isn't just costly—it's fatal.

Remember:

1. You can't scale to eight figures without understanding your financials inside and out..
2. Know your P&L statement. revenue, COGS, gross profit, overhead, and net profit—these aren't just numbers; they're the vital signs of your business. So, go through it with a fine-tooth comb month over month, year over year.
3. Cash flow is king. You can be profitable on paper and still go broke. Track your cash daily and understand where it's coming from and going to.
4. Your balance sheet is your financial health checkup. Know your assets, liabilities, and equity like the back of your hand.
5. Set up performance-based rebates that increase as your purchasing does. You're not trying to fleece anyone—you're trying to create a partnership that benefits everyone.
6. Understand the difference between margin and markup. It can make or break your profitability. Don't let impressive sales numbers blind you to reality.
7. Turn expenses into profit centers. Get creative with your resources and look at every expense as a potential revenue stream.
8. Implement "Profit First." Set aside your profit as soon as money comes in. It forces you to run leanly and efficiently, creating your own rainy day fund.

CHAPTER 5

Strategic Clarity

Next up on our roadmap: strategic clarity. In this chapter, we're going to dissect the art and science of goal setting in business. We're talking short-term goals that keep you on your toes day to day, and long-term goals that push you to think big. Why? Because a business without clear goals is like a ship without a destination. You might be moving, but you're not really going anywhere. This is because goals give your entire team a clear target to aim for, and more importantly, they give you a way to measure your progress.

But setting goals is just the beginning. The real magic happens when you break those goals down into steps with a clear action plan, also known as *The REYG Method (Reverse Engineer Your Goals.)* This method will take your ambitious goals and turn them into daily, weekly, and monthly targets that'll take your business to where you want it to be. Imagine knowing exactly how many sales calls your team needs to make each day to hit your annual revenue target. Or knowing precisely how many new leads, appointments, and customers you need to acquire each month to grow your business by 25 percent this year. That's the power of *REYG*.

We're going to walk through this process step by step together, using real-world examples to show you how it works. You'll learn how to analyze your historical data to set realistic goals, how to break those goals down into manageable chunks, and how to use this information to make smart decisions about everything from hiring to marketing spend. You'll have a clear strategy for not just setting goals, but achieving them. In other words, you'll understand how to create a roadmap that takes you from where you are to where you want to be, with clearly defined milestones along the way. So get ready. We're about to turn your business goals from vague wishes into a clear, strategic plan for success.

REYG: Reverse Engineer Your Goals. It's not just a fancy acronym; it's a game-changer.

Here's how it works: We start with the end goal and work backward. This gives your team crystal clear targets so that everyone knows exactly what they need to do to succeed.

Breaking Down the *REYG* Process

Although *REYG* can be based on things like profit or company valuation, we'll dive into this with a revenue goal as an example.

Say Company A has a revenue goal of $10 million. Sounds great, right? But what does that actually mean in terms of day-to-day operations?

First, we look at their average job or contract value. Let's say it's $10,000. Simple math tells us they need to sell 1,000 contracts over the year to hit that $10 million mark. But we don't stop there. We go deeper. We look at their historical data—preferably three to five years' worth. Why? Because business isn't consistent month to month.

Maybe they sell 5 percent of their yearly revenue in January, but in June, things heat up at 15 percent.

So, for January, they're aiming for $500,000 in sales (5 percent of $10 million). Come June, they need to be hitting $1.5 million (15 percent of $10 million). See how this clarity helps you plan? You know when to ramp up, when you might need extra staff, or when to push marketing harder. More importantly, you know where you need to be based on real data.

Now, I want to tell you about a conversation I've had all too often.

A business owner comes to me and says, "I want to hit $5 million in sales next year." Great goal.

So I ask, "What does your average sales rep sell?"

They say, "$750,000."

"How many sales reps do you have?"

"Two."

I can't help but smile. Two sales reps at $750,000 each is only $1.5 million. To hit $5 million, they need at least seven reps performing at that level. This is the power of *REYG*—it exposes the gaps in your plan before they become problems.

You see, it's not just about setting a big, impressive-sounding goal. It's about understanding exactly what it takes to get there. How many sales reps do you need? How many appointments does each rep need per week? How many calls do they need to make each day?

When you have this level of clarity, big things start to happen. You can make informed decisions about hiring, marketing, everything. Your team knows exactly what's expected of them. Better yet, you can spot problems early—if you're behind in Q1, you know you need to step it up in Q2.

Let's look at *REYG* on a grand scale with Reed Hastings and Netflix.

Back in the late '90s, Hastings had a vision: to create a movie rental service that didn't punish customers with late fees. But he didn't stop there. He reverse engineered the entire process, breaking it down into actionable steps that would eventually disrupt the entire entertainment industry.

Hastings started with the end goal: provide convenient, affordable access to movies without late fees. Then he worked backward. How could they deliver movies to customers without a physical store? The answer was mail delivery. This led to more questions: How many distribution centers would they need? How quickly could they turn around shipments?

Netflix's team crunched the numbers. They calculated how many subscribers they'd need to break even. They figured out how many movies each subscriber would need to rent per month to make the most profitable model. They even calculated the optimal weight for their signature red envelopes to minimize postage costs.

But Hastings was already thinking ahead. He saw that digital streaming was the future, long before broadband internet was widely available. So, he set a new goal: transition Netflix from a DVD-by-mail service to a streaming platform.

Again, he reverse engineered the process. What kind of technology infrastructure would they need? How much bandwidth? How many titles would they need to offer to keep subscribers engaged? What would be the tipping point where streaming became more cost-effective than mailing DVDs?

This approach extended to every level of the company. The content acquisition team had specific targets for how many hours of content they needed to add each month. The tech team had goals for reducing buffering time and improving the recommendation algorithm. The marketing team had targets for subscriber growth and retention rates.

By breaking down these big, ambitious goals into specific, measurable targets, Netflix was able to make informed decisions at every step. They knew exactly what they needed to achieve and by when. This method allowed Netflix to pivot successfully from DVDs to streaming, and then to producing their own content.

In 2013, when they released *House of Cards*, their first major original series, it wasn't a shot in the dark. They had reverse engineered the process, using data on viewer preferences to inform their content strategy.

It's not just about having a vision—it's about understanding exactly what it takes to turn that vision into reality. Whether you're aiming to disrupt an industry or hit your first eight figures in revenue, the principle is the same: Start with the end goal, then work backward to create a step-by-step plan to get there.

Deep Dive

If you're running a company where your sales reps are running leads instead of generating them, you need to know their close rate like it's your social security number. Why? Because this number is the key to understanding how many leads you need to hit your sales targets.

Let's explore what this means for sales reps:

Say you've set your sights on $5 million in revenue. First things first, what's your average job? If it's $10,000, you will need to sell 500 contracts to hit that $5 million goal. Now, let's say your sales team is closing at 33 percent across the board. That's not too shabby, but it means you need to run 1,500 appointments to close those 500 deals. But wait, we're not done yet. What percent of leads convert into appointments (your lead-to-appointment rate)? If it's 50 percent, then you need 3,000 leads to make this whole machine work.

In other words:

1. You start with 3,000 leads.
2. Fifty percent of those convert to appointments, giving you 1,500 appointments.
3. You close a third of those appointments, landing you 500 new clients.
4. Five hundred contracts at $10,000 each puts $5 million in your pocket.

So, you need to generate 3,000 leads to hit your goal. See how that works? Good!

Pay attention because here's where a lot of businesses drop the ball.

If we break this down even further and look at it month by month, we know from our historical data mentioned above that January typically accounts for 5 percent of our annual business. What does this mean for our January targets?

Well, 5 percent of 3,000 leads is 150. So, in January, you need to generate 150 leads. If everything goes according to plan, those 150 leads should turn into 75 appointments (remember, 50 percent lead-to-appointment rate), which should result in about 25 closed contracts (33 percent close rate) at $10,000 a pop, or $250,000 in revenue for January.

Now, do this for each month and show your team at the beginning of each month what you must hit to achieve your annual goals.

Next, let's reverse engineer things all the way down to lead costs. If you know it costs you $100 to generate a lead, then you're looking at a $300,000 investment in lead generation to reach 3,000 leads to hit your $5 million goal. Is that within your budget? Can you ramp up month over month to achieve that? If not, you might need to look at ways to lower your lead costs or improve your conversion rates.

Finally, let's talk about customer acquisition costs (CAC). CAC is crucial because it tells you what levers you can pull to grow your company efficiently. Knowing your CAC can help you look at ways to lower your lead costs, convert more leads into appointments, improve upon your close rate, and even make decisions when it comes to raising your prices. For example, if it's costing you $2,000 to acquire a customer on a $10,000 job, that's a 20 percent CAC, and it's eating into your profit margins big time. You need to get crystal clear on what your customer acquisition costs need to be as a percentage of your revenue.

The point is, when you reverse engineer your goals like this, you're not just shooting in the dark. You're creating a precise roadmap for success. You know exactly what you need to do each day, each week, and each month to hit your targets and hit the next level.

REYG Example for Business Owners

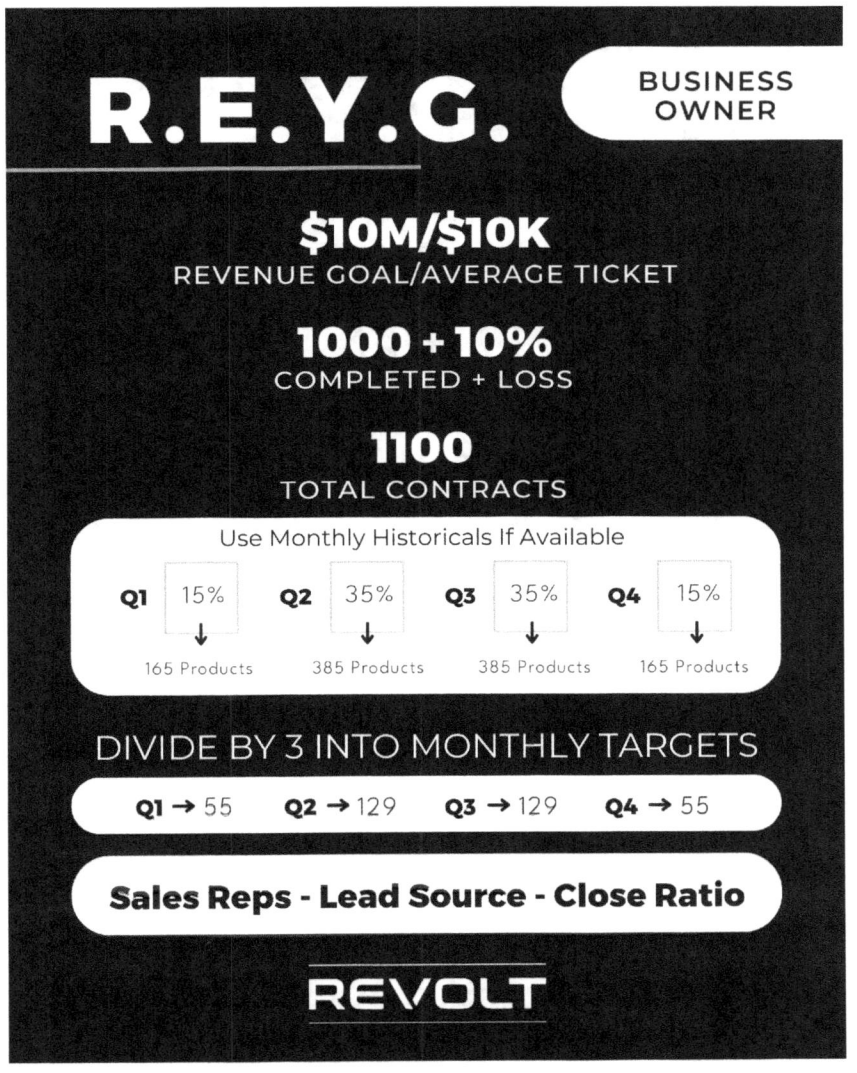

REYG Example for Sales Reps

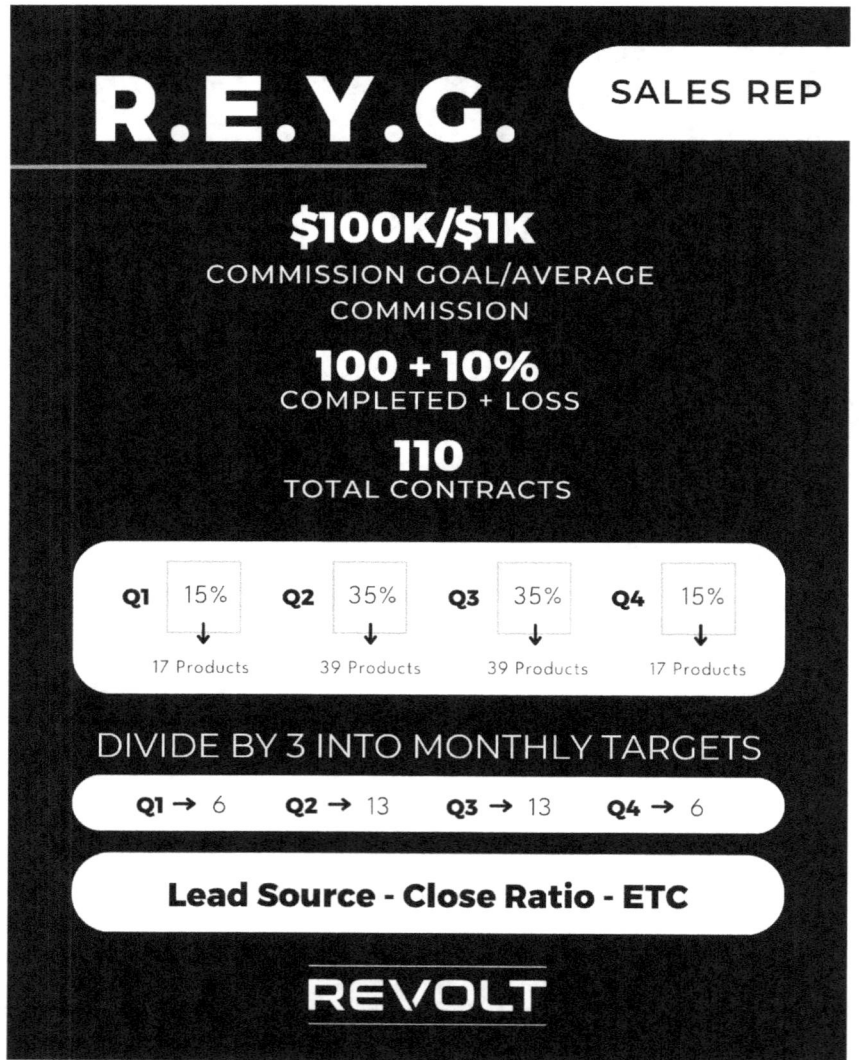

Starting With Profit

What if we used profit instead of revenue? The breakdown is much the same, but the numbers change.

Say you want to make $1 million in net profit. Great goal, but how do you get there? It all depends on your net profit margin. Let's break it down:

- If you're netting 20 percent, you need $5 million in revenue.
- If you're only netting 5 percent, you're looking at $20 million in revenue.
- At 10 percent net profit, you need $10 million in revenue.

See how that works? By starting with your desired profit, you get a much clearer picture of what your revenue needs to be. It's not about chasing a flashy top-line number—it's about building a sustainable, profitable business.

The *REYG* Method in Action

If you want to achieve $1 million in net profit on $10 million in revenue, that leaves you with a net margin of 10 percent. You must monitor your COGS and overhead to ensure you don't overspend. If you do, you'll be left with less than 10 percent and will not hit your goal.

Goal: $10 million in revenue
Average job: $10,000
Target: 1,000 contracts

We need to know our numbers at every stage of the sales process:

1. Close rate: 33 percent
2. Lead-to-appointment rate: 50 percent

Working backward:

- 1,000 contracts at $10,000 each = $10 million.
- To get 1,000 contracts at a 33 percent close rate, we need 3000 appointments.
- To get 3,000 appointments at a 50 percent lead-to-appointment rate, we need 6,000 leads.

Now, we know our magic number: 6,000 leads. But we're not done yet. Remember how we talked about using historical data? Let's apply that here.

If January typically accounts for 5 percent of your annual business:

- Five percent of 6,000 leads = 300 leads needed in January.
- This should translate to 150 appointments (50 percent conversion).
- Which should result in about 50 contracts (33 percent close rate).
- At $10,000 per contract, that's $500,000 in revenue for January.

See how powerful this is? We've taken a big, annual goal and broken it down into monthly, even daily, targets. Your team isn't just chasing a vague $10 million goal—they know exactly how many leads, appointments, and contracts they need each month to get there.

Let's look at how Ray Dalio, founder of Bridgewater Associates, applies a similar principle. Dalio is famous for his "goals to tasks" approach, which is essentially *REYG*.

He starts with the ultimate goal, then works backward to determine what needs to happen at each stage to achieve that goal. For instance, when Dalio set out to build Bridgewater into a world-class investment firm, he didn't just focus on the end goal. He broke it down into specific milestones:

1. Develop a unique investment strategy.
2. Build a team of top-tier analysts.
3. Create a robust risk management system.
4. Establish a strong track record of returns.

Each of these milestones was further broken down into specific tasks and targets. This approach allowed Dalio and his team to always know exactly what they needed to do next to move closer to their ultimate goal.

Dalio's method, like *REYG*, is all about creating clarity. You need to understand exactly what it takes to get there, and then break that down into daily, actionable steps.

REYG With Your Team

It's time to take this *REYG* method and apply it to your sales team. Instead of just throwing out company goals in your next meeting with your sales reps, flip the script and ask them, "What are your income goals?" If you've done *The Six Bricks* exercise with them, then you know what drives them, and can encourage them to build financial goals based on their results from the exercise. This isn't just small talk—it's the first step in empowering your team to take control of their success.

Let's say one of your reps pipes up and says they want to make $100,000 this year. Great goal, right? But how do we get there? This is where *REYG* comes in.

You know that your average commission is $2,000 per contract. So, let's do some quick math:

$100,000 goal ÷ $2,000 per contract = 50 contracts

Just like that, you've given your rep a clear target and not some vague notion of "sell more."

If broken down evenly, it turns into:

- Quarterly goal: twelve to thirteen contracts
- Monthly goal: four to five contracts
- Weekly goal: one to two contracts

Now, your rep isn't just looking at a mountain of fifty contracts to climb. They've got manageable, bite-sized goals to hit each week.

Next, let's look at how your rep generates leads. Are they a "lead baby," relying on the company to feed them leads, or are they a self-generator?

If they're relying on company leads, we need to know their close rate. Let's say it's 25 percent. That means to close fifty contracts, they need to run 200 appointments. If the company's lead-to-appointment rate is 50 percent, that means we need to feed this rep 400 leads over the year.

But what if the rep is a self-generator? That's a whole different ball game, and we need to dig into their lead generation methods:

- Door-to-Door: How many doors do they need to knock on to get one lead?

- Digital Marketing: What's their conversion rate on social media posts?
- Facebook Groups: How many posts or interactions lead to one solid lead?
- Networking Groups: How many events do they need to attend to generate X number of leads?

By breaking it down this way, you're not just giving your rep a goal—you're giving them a roadmap to success. They know exactly what they need to do each day, each week, each month to hit their income goal. Also, it's not just about hitting company targets anymore. They're not just working for a paycheck. They're working toward their own goals. It's personal because this process turns your sales reps from employees into entrepreneurs within your business. Now they're not just along for the ride but in the driver's seat of their own success.

Remember, a team of self-motivated, goal-oriented reps isn't just good for them—it's good for your bottom line. When they win, you win. This is how you build a sales team that doesn't just meet targets—they smash them and propel your business to that eight-figure mark and beyond.

Clarity Calculator

The perfect partner to *REYG* is the *Clarity Calculator*, which gives you a clear direction forward and is powered by cold, hard data.

Access The *Clarity Calculator* Here: TheRevolt.com/roadmap

Here's how it works. You plug in your goals along with custom inputs, and it spits out exactly how many appointments you need, how many leads you've got to generate, and can even give you a ballpark valuation of your company based on what multiple you believe you can achieve.

Now, I'll be straight with you—that last part involves a bit of educated guesswork based on industry multiples, but hey, it's a heck of a lot better than flying blind, right?

Here's how I use it in real-life examples. Say I want my plumbing business to do $100 million in revenue per year in Travelers Rest, South Carolina. I love my hometown, but with a population of 8,000, there aren't enough toilets in Travelers Rest to support that kind of revenue. The *Clarity Calculator* really helps us get clear on what it would actually take to hit that $100 million mark. Let's run the numbers:

- Goal: $100 million
- Average ticket cost: $5,000
- Jobs per month: 1,600
- Jobs per year: 20,000

Okay, is that number realistic in my market? *No!* It isn't realistic to run 1,600 jobs per month in that small of a market. So, let's start looking at how many markets we need to hit that goal. We're talking major metropolitan areas: Atlanta, Nashville, Charlotte, and Raleigh. These are cities with populations in the millions, where thousands of jobs a year per location starts to look realistic.

The *Clarity Calculator* forces you to face reality. It's like a bucket of cold water to the face of your dreams—not to drown them, but to let you know what hard questions need to be answered: How many locations do I really need? What markets can support my growth goals? How do I need to divide my resources to make this happen?

This isn't about crushing your dreams. It's about giving them a solid foundation in reality. Because, let me tell you, there's nothing more disappointing than chasing a goal for years only to realize it was never achievable in the first place.

With the *Clarity Calculator*, you're not just dreaming big—you're dreaming smart. You're taking that $100 million goal and breaking it down into actionable steps across multiple markets. You're not just saying, "I want to build a huge business." You're saying, "I'm going to build a $20 million operation in Atlanta, another in Nashville, another in Charlotte, and so on."

So, help yourself by turning vague aspirations into concrete plans, allocating your resources effectively, planning your expansion strategically, and setting realistic targets for each of your locations.

Best Practices For Setting Realistic Yet Ambitious Goals

To recap, *REYG* (Reverse Engineer Your Goals) is your secret weapon here. It helps you outline your path, showing you exactly what you have to do. Couple it with our *Clarity Calculator* as well as *The Six Bricks* exercise for personal goals, and you've got a recipe for success. It just comes down to are you going to do it or not?

This isn't just important for you as the business owner; it's vital for your team members too. Get crystal clear on what they want out of life. Know their intentions. Why? Because if you help them hit their goals, they'll be loyal to you and help you hit yours. It's that simple.

How can you maintain focus on long-term goals? You've got to talk about your goals often. Not just with yourself but with your team. Get everyone laser focused on the goals.

Remember when we talked about a common mission earlier in the book? That's key here. When you have a common mission, when you're all working toward something bigger than yourselves or the company—something that's not just about profit but about helping others—it gives everyone a reason to push forward even when things get tough.

Moving the Goalpost

Now, here's a question I get a lot, "Is moving the goalpost bad for morale?"

Here's my take: If you set the standard from the get-go that "we're always going to be evolving, and we're always going to be moving the goalpost to become better," then it becomes part of your culture.

It's all about mindset. If your team understands that growth and improvement are constant, then moving the goalpost isn't demoralizing—it's an exciting new challenge to tackle.

Setting and achieving goals isn't a one-time thing. It's an ongoing process. It's about constant improvement, constant clarity, and constant communication. We're not in the business of being average. In fact, we're downright *against average*.

If you're serious about building an eight-figure business, you don't want to be stagnant or attract people to the company who are okay with being stagnant. You want positive people who embrace change, and understand that you're always going to be moving forward, adapting, and trying to get better. Because this isn't just a mindset—it's who we are at our core. It's the DNA of our company and you should adapt this mindset too if you want to hit those ambitious goals we've been talking about.

Now, you might be wondering, *Hunter, how do we keep this momentum going? How do we reboot mentally when we hit our goals?* Great question. Here's what works for us:

1. Annual Retreats: These aren't just about training. They're about having fun, getting to know each other better, becoming friends with the people you work with, and building a team that becomes a family. With Revolt, we even offer services where we help you plan and lead the retreat if you aren't comfortable doing it yourself or would like a third party to handle it.

2. Family Events: Getting to know the team's families by hosting family events at the office isn't just feel-good fluff. When your team's families buy into your mission, your team becomes even more committed. Rent inflatables, bring food, have fun!

3. Weekly Meetings: This is where you're working together to improve consistently. It's about keeping that momentum going, week after week.

As we wrap up this chapter on strategic clarity and goal setting, I want you to remember one thing: Your goals are only as good as the team working toward them.

We've talked about setting clear, ambitious goals. We've discussed how to reverse engineer those goals and create a roadmap to success. But none of that matters if you don't have the right people on your team. In the next chapter, we're going to dive deep into recruiting and retaining top talent. Because, let's face it—in the world of eight-figure businesses, your team is everything.

Remember:

1. Strategic clarity isn't just about setting goals; it's about creating a clear action plan to turn your business aspirations into reality.

2. Use the *REYG* (Reverse Engineer Your Goals) method to break down big goals into actionable daily, weekly, and monthly targets.

3. For informed decision-making, understand your numbers inside and out—from average job value to close rates and lead generation costs.

4. Start with profit goals, not just revenue, for a clearer picture of what your revenue needs to be for sustainable growth.

5. Use tools like the *Clarity Calculator* to face reality and ensure your goals are ambitious yet achievable in your market.

6. Create a culture of constant improvement where "moving the goalpost" is seen as an exciting challenge, not a burden. Regular team events and communication are key to maintaining this momentum.

CHAPTER 6

Recruiting Top Talent

Whether I'm leading a retreat, speaking on stage, or a business owner is flying out for the one-on-one Legacy Day I offer at my office, recruiting is typically one of the top hurdles I hear about. This is a problem because, after consulting thousands of business owners, I can say with confidence that recruiting top talent might just be the single most valuable building block to an eight-figure business. So, in this chapter, we won't just talk about filling seats; we'll talk about building a dream team that'll take your business to the top.

To do this, we'll get into specific details—answering questions like, "How do I know when to hire for each role?"—explore techniques, and devise strategies on talent acquisition; build a recruiting funnel that will save you time by making your company the go-to destination for top talent; and dive into leveraging different sources to find those hungry individuals who aren't just looking for a job, but a mission.

By the end of this chapter, you'll have the tools to ensure that even your weakest link is strong enough to support your eight-figure dreams. But let me be straight—there isn't some one-size-fits-all formula. It's very dependent on your market and the current state of your company.

The Recruiting Roadmap

Let's get into the specifics on hiring. If you're an owner-operator and still involved in the business, I always recommend that you focus on hiring people that cost you little to no money while also bringing in more money. What role am I talking about? Sales reps.

Many times the key to unlocking and scaling up to eight figures is about hiring sales reps that are hungry, match your culture, and will go out and sell for your company. This is because a sales rep is not just an employee but a growth engine you only have to fuel when it's already producing cash. How? If you hire sales reps as commission-only team members, you will quickly realize that the beauty of the commission-only structure is that it attracts the hungriest, most motivated individuals out there. So, start by hiring sales reps as you manage the back end, because if you want to grow you need to focus on bringing in cash—I cannot emphasize this enough. Then, as your revenue grows from your sales reps, begin to hire for the back end.

Once you've got your sales machine humming along, you're going to find yourself with some extra cash. Now, many business owners think they need to hire a high-level operations person or maybe even treat themselves to a fancy new car. I think it's a mistake to think like this. Instead, what you want to do is consider an office manager as the next hire. Why? Because an office manager is not only like the Swiss Army knife of your business, but they're your right-hand person. They can answer the phones, set leads, order materials, schedule laborers, talk to clients after you've sold the job, and if you hire the right person, they can even help with small bookkeeping tasks or help manage the financial service provider.

The lesson: You have probably heard the old saying, "Hire fast; fire fast," and sure, there's some truth to that. However, I do believe with certain positions you are much better off taking the time needed to find the exact fit. So, be strategic; don't just grab the first warm body that walks through the door.

This isn't a sprint; it's a marathon. Take your time and make sure that you set the right expectations. Start outlining all the tasks you feel they could take off of your plate in great detail—even if that means cleaning the toilet—and make sure you have a team player that's willing to do whatever it takes. Why? Because if you don't, you're setting yourself up for a world of hurt down the road. This is where the funnel will help.

Now, let's say you've got your office manager in place and your business is still growing. What's next? As you start to grow even more in revenue and jobs, then you hire a production manager. The production manager's primary concern is whether or not the actual product is being delivered. This is the person who's going to free up more of your and the office manager's time. Some tasks they may take on include: scheduling the jobs with homeowners, ordering the materials, scheduling the labor, going out and making sure the job's done right, and doing a quality control (QC) check.

These are just the first few key hires that can take your business to eight figures and beyond. Beyond these first few roles, you'll start to build out the org chart with marketing, finance, and so on. Just remember, it's about strategic growth: putting the right people in the right positions at the right time.

Crystallizer Assessment

As you continue to grow your business, you'll find that there are many positions to fill between your initial hires and your full-fledged leadership team. But as you build out the baseline of your team—

from salespeople to office manager to production—you'll eventually need to hire someone to handle operations. Not just the operations of your projects but the operations of the company itself.

Whether you need this operations person right away depends largely on your own strengths and weaknesses, which is where the Crystallizer Assessment comes in. The Crystallizer Assessment is a free test by Gino Wickman that can be found online. As we get into this part, I think it's important that you take this assessment yourself. This isn't just some personality quiz you'd find in a magazine. This is a powerful tool that can help you understand your leadership style and what kind of support you need. The Crystallizer Assessment will tell you if you're more of a "Visionary" or an "Integrator." If you haven't done it already, take the assessment before moving on.

What's your result?

Visionary: _____
Integrator: _____

A Visionary is the big ideas person. They're the ones setting goals, talking to the people that have the bigger relationships and bigger clients inside the company. Visionaries are great at seeing the big picture and charting the course for the company's future. They're often the face of the company, and can inspire others with their passion and drive.

Ideal jobs for Visionaries might include:

- CEO or Founder of a Startup
- Chief Innovation Officer
- Brand Strategist

On the flip side, an Integrator is the one building out your company's systems and processes, managing people, tracking KPIs, holding people accountable, and doing the day-to-day detailed work that the visionary is not good at. They're the ones who take the Visionary's big ideas and turn them into action plans as they keep the ship on course day in and day out.

Ideal jobs for Integrators might include:

- Chief Operating Officer (COO)
- Operations Manager
- Office Manager

Many times owners and founders that start the company are Visionaries and they're not good at the day-to-day. If that sounds like you, don't worry—you're in good company. Some of the most successful businesses in the world were built by Visionaries who had the self-awareness to bring on strong Integrators to balance them out.

Understanding whether you're a Visionary or an Integrator isn't just about putting a label on yourself. It's about recognizing your strengths and weaknesses, and building a team that complements your skills. If you're a Visionary, you're likely going to need that operations person—that Integrator—to come in and help you out. They'll be the one to take your big ideas and turn them into reality, and keep the trains running on time while you're out there dreaming up the next big thing. On the other hand, if you're an Integrator, you might not need to hire this role as quickly because you might be able to handle both the big picture and the day-to-day operations for a while longer. The key here is self-awareness.

There's no right or wrong here. The world needs both Visionaries and Integrators. The most successful businesses are often those that have both working in harmony. So, use the Crystallizer Assessment's knowledge to build the best team for your business.

Hiring Smarter

Back in 2018, I was a year into growing Cornerstone Construction and was as green as they came. I didn't know anything about construction or roofing. But I had the good sense to hire a sales rep who knew the roofing industry inside and out. This guy was a smart hire - he was helping with operations, sales, you name it. Meanwhile, I was just focused on generating leads.

Here's where I made a mistake. I got stubborn. I was telling our sales reps that we didn't need to knock on doors. In my infinite wisdom, I thought we could just run ads and the leads would come pouring in.

One day, a kid walks in looking for a job. He says he's been following us on social media and likes what we're doing. During the interview, I asked him how he typically got his leads. His response? "Well, I knock on doors."

Now, remember, I'm Mr. "We Don't Need to Knock Doors" at this point. So I tell him, "Okay, well, you don't have to do that here."

To which the kid asked, "Well, can I if I still want to?"

I figured, what the heck, and told him, "Sure, if that's what you want to do."

Little did I know this decision was about to turn our whole operation on its head. In his first month, this kid sold $250,000 in business. Let that sink in for a minute. Up until then, we hadn't had a single rep sell more than $100,000 in a month. Talk about a reality check. I had to swallow my pride and admit I was dead wrong. It was as clear as day that we needed to focus on teaching the rest of our guys how to knock doors. Here's the real kicker: this wasn't just about boosting our sales numbers. It opened my eyes to what was truly possible. We could bring in other sales reps and give them the opportunity to change their lives by knocking doors too.

This realization was a game-changer. It wasn't just about growing our company anymore. It was about creating opportunities for people to transform their lives. We quickly shifted gears and started figuring out how to train these reps effectively. (We'll dive deep into training in the next chapter!)

Don't let your ego or preconceived notions hold you back. Be open to ideas from your team, especially those who might have different experiences or perspectives. Remember, if you're the smartest person in the room, you're in the wrong room.

This kid who walked in off the street? He schooled me. And I'm dang grateful he did. It changed the trajectory of our entire business.

When you're building your team, look for people who can teach you something. Look for those who challenge your thinking and push you out of your comfort zone. Because those are the people who will help take your business to the next level.

And always, always be willing to admit when you're wrong. It's not a sign of weakness - it's a sign of strength and adaptability. In the world of business, those who can't adapt get left behind.

Again, the goal isn't to be the smartest person in the room. The goal is to build a team of smart people who can help you achieve your vision.

Recruiting Funnel

Some of you might be thinking, *What the heck is a recruiting funnel?* It's the key to recruiting top talent, and a shortcut that'll save you hundreds of hours every single year. Trust me on this one.

First off, you're going to need some software. You could use something like GoHighLevel, ClickFunnels, Leadpages, or even WordPress. The software doesn't matter as much as the structure. The structure is key here.

Now, I hear you… "I'm not tech savvy."

You don't have to be. You can hire someone to build it for you for a fraction of the money it will make you. But first, let me break it down for you.

Picture this: A potential recruit lands on your funnel page. Right at the top, they're greeted with a simple prompt, "Hey, please watch these two videos, and then afterward, you can apply below."

The first video is all about the position you're hiring for. If it's a sales gig, we're talking sales. If it's for an assistant, we're diving into what it means to be an assistant in your company. If it's for the COO position, we're breaking down what it means to help lead the charge.

This is what makes the process different. The first half of that video we're not pulling any punches. We're laying out all the "bad" stuff.

Anything someone might see as negative, we're putting it front and center. Why? Because we want to weed out the tire-kickers and time-wasters.

Say we're hiring for a sales rep at my roofing company. In that first half of the video, I'm going to say something like, "Hey, listen up. If you're afraid of heights, this job is not for you. You'll be climbing ladders and walking on roofs. If knocking doors and talking to strangers makes you sweat, well, you might want to look elsewhere. Also, if you're not okay with being a commission-only employee, hit that back button right now." In other words, I'm laying it all out, the good, the bad, and the ugly, by telling them straight up, "If this doesn't sound like your cup of tea, no hard feelings. Just click off the video. We're not a good fit."

Same for my assistant. I'll tell them there may be days I need them to clean my house for a party or take my truck for an oil change. I've even told them one of the duties is to clean my crapper weekly because I want to make sure they're all in and not afraid to get their hands dirty.

Now, what about the second half of that video?

If they make it through that gauntlet, this is when we start selling the dream. We're talking about how awesome the company is, the quality of our product, and our killer customer experience. We're painting a picture of the company's vision, showing them exactly how much they can make, giving them a clear roadmap to hitting their goals with us, and all the opportunity that resides ahead.

Next up, we've got a second video for them. This one is all about the foundation of the company. We're talking vision, mission, and core values. We're also showing off what we do in the community, our common mission. Why? Because we're not just selling a job; we're interviewing for a place in our family.

This two-video approach is pure gold because it does two things:

1. It weeds out the people who aren't a good fit before anyone wastes time with an application or interview.
2. It gets potential recruits excited about your company. By the time they hit that apply button, they're not just looking for a job—they're looking to be part of something bigger.

Let's look at Grant Cardone, real estate mogul and sales trainer. Where it concerns hiring, Cardone said, "I don't hire people who need a job; I hire people who want to be part of building something great." This means hiring people who are aligned with the company's mission and are willing to go above and beyond for that mission.

Alex Hormozi, founder of Gym Launch and acquisition.com, also had a nugget of wisdom to share regarding hiring. Hormozi said, "Hire for hunger; train for skill," which means you can teach skills, but you can't teach drive. To better demonstrate this, Hormozi shared a story about hiring a salesperson who had no sales experience but had an insatiable hunger to succeed. This person ended up outperforming seasoned sales professionals because of their determination and willingness to learn.

When you get people applying who are already bought into your vision and excited about your company, that's when the sparks fly. Again, recruiting isn't just about filling seats with warm bodies. It's about finding the right people to help you on the journey of building your legacy.

When candidates finish watching your videos, it's time for them to move on to the application. Now, depending on the position, you'll have different questions, but for a sales position, we're looking at some key information that goes beyond their basic personal information and past experience—their personality assessment.

Remember earlier how I mentioned that collecting data is key? Having our team members take a personality assessment and storing this information as data has allowed us to learn which personalities work best for what role.

Within my businesses, we swear by 16personalities.com. After using it hundreds of times, we've seen firsthand how it helps us find the right fit for our team. This is because it doesn't just give you a label; it provides insights into a person's motivations, strengths, and potential areas for growth.

The assessment offered by 16personalities.com is based on the Myers-Briggs Type Indicator (MBTI), and is designed to be user-friendly and accessible. The test categorizes people into sixteen distinct personality types, each with its own unique blend of traits. These types are based on four dimensions:

1. Extraversion (E) vs. Introversion (I)
2. Sensing (S) vs. Intuition (N)
3. Thinking (T) vs. Feeling (F)
4. Judging (J) vs. Perceiving (P)

I didn't know which personality fit where when we started. But because of collecting this data and looking back, we have a shortcut that can prevent us from wasting time putting the wrong people in a certain role. We've learned through experience and studying the data, who fit where, and who didn't fit at all. Which personality type I worked well with or didn't, and which ones fit well in our company culture. When it comes to sales, we've found that the Protagonist (ENFJ) personality type often shines. These folks are like the charismatic leaders you see in movies—they're inspiring, passionate, and genuinely care about others. These traits are gold for a sales role because they can connect with customers on a deep level, truly understand their needs, and sell with conviction because they believe in what they're offering.

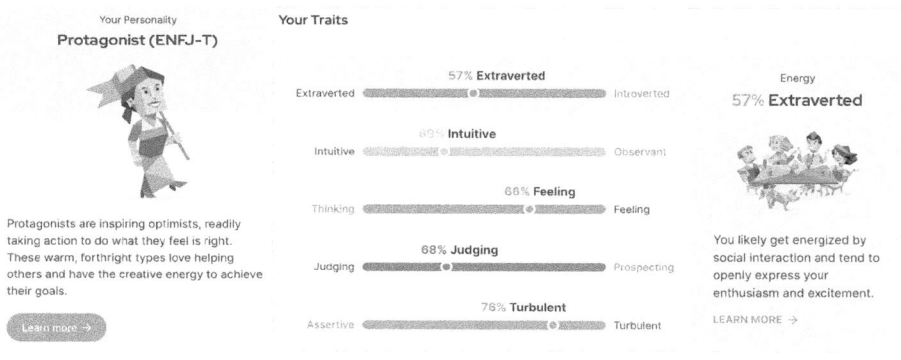

Protagonists aren't just great at sales. Their natural leadership and people skills make them ideal for a variety of roles:

1. Sales Representative: Obviously, this is their strong suit.
2. Marketing Manager: They can craft compelling messages that resonate with audiences.
3. Human Resources Specialist: Their empathy and communication skills are perfect for managing people.
4. Teacher or Trainer: They excel at inspiring and motivating others to learn.

5. Nonprofit Organizer: Their passion for causes makes them great at rallying support.

While Protagonists are often our go-to for sales roles, don't forget about other personality types that could be a perfect fit for different aspects of your business:

1. The Entrepreneur (ESTP): These are your bold, energetic types. They're quick on their feet and excel at spotting and seizing opportunities. They'd be perfect as:
    o   Business Development Managers: They're always on the lookout for the next big deal.
    o   Real Estate Agents: Their energy and people skills are perfect for showing properties.
    o   Stockbrokers: They thrive in fast-paced, high-stakes environments.

2. The Executive (ESTJ): If you need someone to keep things running smoothly, look no further. These folks are excellent administrators, unmatched at managing both tasks and people. They'd excel as:
    o   Operations Managers: They can keep your business running like a well-oiled machine.
    o   Project Managers: Their organizational skills ensure projects are completed on time and on budget.
    o   Financial Planners: Their attention to detail and logical thinking make them great with numbers.

3. The Consul (ESFJ): These are your people persons. They're outgoing, caring, and have an uncanny ability to remember personal details. They're perfect for roles like:
    o   Customer Service Representatives: They'll make your customers feel heard and valued.

- o Public Relations Specialists: Their networking skills can help build and maintain your company's image.
- o Event Planners: They excel at coordinating people and details to create memorable experiences.

We're not just looking for skills—we're looking for the right personality traits, the right mindset, the right "hunger for success."

Remember, the goal isn't to find perfect people. It's to find the right people for the right roles. By understanding personality types and what drives different individuals, you can create a team that's not just skilled, but passionate, motivated, and aligned with your company's mission. So, as you build your team, don't just look at resumes. Dig deeper. Use tools like 16personalities.com to understand what makes your candidates tick. Because with the right personalities in the right roles, there's no limit to what you can achieve.

Now, back to our recruitment process. After the candidate has watched both videos and taken the personality test, we inquire about their work experience and ask for their social media profile links, which gives us a chance to check them out before we invest any more time.

From there, we usually allow them to schedule a phone interview. This initial screening is typically handled by someone on our team, not the owner or operator (unless you're still a small operation).

Here is a list of the questions we ask them:

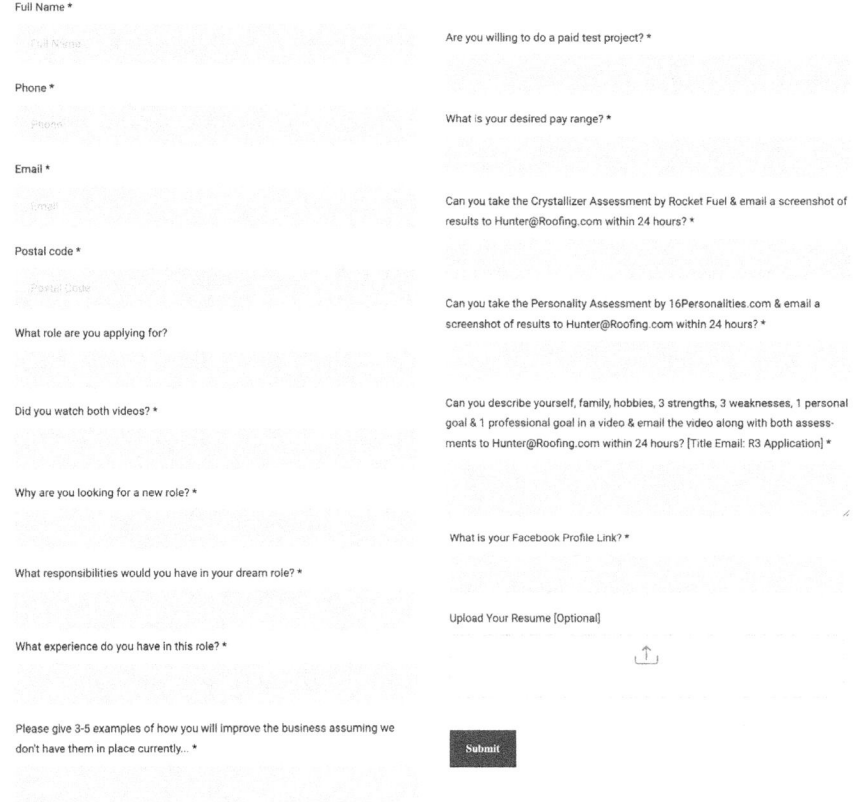

If the phone interview goes well, we move to an in-person interview with someone from our leadership team. At this point, we're pretty confident they're a good fit—we're just confirming our impressions and answering any final questions they might have. This may seem like a long process, but that's kind of the point. If a candidate makes it through to this point, they are committed and truly interested in joining your team.

Access The Recruiting Funnel Here: TheRevolt.com/roadmap

Where do we use the Recruiting Funnel?

The recruiting funnel is designed to work whether you're a one-person show or a growing enterprise and can save you hundreds of hours, especially if you're trying to hire reps quickly. We've gotten over a thousand applicants in a single year through platforms like ZipRecruiter, Indeed, LinkedIn, and Facebook.

Many owners get stressed, questioning what the ad should say, what responsibilities should be listed, and so on. Leveraging ChatGPT and other AI tools can eliminate any fears you have. Just give it good prompts such as, "write a job description with clear responsibilities and expectations for our new sales reps" or "create a list of KPIs that our new sales rep must achieve." The job of AI is simply to do 90 percent of the work, so all you have to do is the last 10 percent.

Once you get your text ready, don't limit yourself to job boards. Get active on social media platforms. Use Facebook ads and Facebook groups; I'm talking about industry groups, local business groups, entrepreneurship groups—anywhere your ideal candidates might be hanging out. Start engaging, sharing your story, talking about your company culture. Even reach out to past customers—offer a finder's fee if they help you hire someone. You'd be surprised how many great candidates you can find just by being active and visible on social media.

Get your current sales reps and team members involved in recruiting. We've even implemented a leadership program where we incentivize our current reps to recruit and train new hires. We offer them a percentage of the new hire's sales for a year, as long as they help lead and train them. It's a win-win—we get new talent, and our current reps are motivated to ensure the new hires succeed.

If you're looking to take your recruitment to the next level, you might want to consider a done-for-you service. We use KRUTR to recruit for us, and they have done a great job handling the entire front end of the recruitment process. They're out there hustling, finding top talent, doing initial screenings, and only sending the cream of the crop your way. This means you're not wasting time sifting through hundreds of resumes or conducting countless preliminary interviews. You're only dealing with pre-qualified candidates who have a high likelihood of being a great fit for your company. All you have to do is show up for the interviews, which frees you up to focus on what you do best—running your business and driving growth.

If you're not yet in a position to hire out this part, take the earlier ideas and put them to use. Never underestimate the power of social media, word of mouth, and incentivizing your team.

Access Our Go-To DFY Recruiting Service Here: TheRevolt.com/roadmap

Recap

Let's wrap this up by breaking down the stages of an effective recruitment funnel. This is the roadmap that's going to take you from attracting talent to watching them become key players in your eight-figure organization.

1. Video One: Role and Responsibilities: This is where you lay it all out—the good, the bad, and the ugly. Be honest about what the job entails.
2. Video Two: Company Overview: Sell the dream. Talk about your vision, your culture, and your impact.
3. Application: Get the basics, but also dig deeper with personality assessments and probing questions.

4. Team Testimonials: List videos of your team members talking about the company on the funnel.

5. Phone Interview: Your first real-time interaction. Use this to gauge their communication skills and enthusiasm.

6. In-Person Interview: This is where you really get to know them. Assess cultural fit and dive deep into their experience.

7. Onboarding: Welcome them to the team and set them up for success.

8. Training: Equip them with the knowledge and skills they need to excel.

9. Performance and Growth: Watch them crush it and become a key member of your team.

This allows you to recruit with confidence, and to promise potential hires that you'll set them up for success when you look them in the eye and say, "We're going to give you the tools, the training, the technology to win. But *you've* got to show up. *You've* got to put in the work." This is crucial, folks. If you know in your heart that you're equipping your team well and someone doesn't make it, then you know it's not because you failed them—they failed themselves.

As we wrap up this chapter on recruitment, I want you to remember one thing: The team you build today is the foundation of your eight-figure business tomorrow; so take the time to get it right, and don't settle for anyone less.

When it comes to building your team, we're just getting started. At the next stop on our roadmap, we're going to dive into how to train and retain this top talent you've just recruited. Because getting them in the door is only half the battle—keeping them engaged, motivated, and performing at their peak is the real mark of success.

Remember:

1. Start by hiring sales reps, ideally on a commission-only basis, to fuel growth without immediate overhead costs.
2. Use the Crystallizer Assessment to understand if you're a Visionary or Integrator, and hire accordingly to complement your strengths.
3. Always aim to hire people smarter than you—they'll challenge your thinking and help take your business to the next level.
4. Implement a recruiting funnel to save time and attract candidates who are already aligned with your company's vision and culture.
5. Leverage personality assessments like 16personalities.com to find the right fit for different roles in your organization.
6. Don't limit your recruitment efforts to job boards—use social media, referrals, and even consider outsourcing to services like KRUTR.
7. Provide candidates with a clear, honest picture of both the challenges and opportunities of the role—this helps weed out poor fits and attracts those who are truly committed.

CHAPTER 7

Train and Retain

In this chapter, we're going to unlock the tricks of building a team that doesn't just perform, but consistently outperforms. We're talking about fostering a culture of continuous improvement that's going to take your business from good to great, and then from great to completely unstoppable. We're going to explore why continuous improvement is the heartbeat of any eight-figure business; we'll dive into techniques for developing a growth-oriented team culture that'll have your competitors wondering what your secret is; and we're going to hammer home why training is absolutely crucial if you want to retain top talent for years to come.

In January 2019, that kid who generated $250,000 in his first month from door knocking really drove home the importance of training for me. It made me think, *If we could train others to do exactly what this kid did, we could help them hit their goals, change their lives, and transform their families' futures.* This realization lit a fire under me, and I started to build what I call the *Six-Figure Blueprint.* It's a custom-built platform designed specifically for Cornerstone Construction, but it has also helped thousands of business owners worldwide through our retreats and conferences.

I'm going to share this blueprint with you today because if you use it—really use it—it works. The whole point of *Six-Figure Blueprint* was to show our sales reps how to make six figures. We're talking about taking someone with zero sales experience, zero product knowledge, and turning them into a six-figure earner. Now, your "Company University" doesn't just have to be for sales reps. You can include other roles, but for the purpose of this chapter, I will explain how to build it out for sales reps.

Here's what makes the *Six-Figure Blueprint* so powerful:

1. Comprehensive Training: We cover everything from the core values, mission and vision of the company, to basics of sales, the intricacies of our specific industry, and how to use our CRM from start to finish. No stone is left unturned.

2. Step-by-Step Guidance: We break our process into manageable, actionable steps. There's no guesswork involved.

3. Continuous Learning: This isn't a one-and-done program. We've built in ongoing education to keep our reps at the top of their game.

4. Practical Application: We don't just teach theory. We show our reps how to apply what they've learned in real-world situations.

5. Measurable Goals: We set clear, achievable milestones so our reps can see their progress and stay motivated.

With this program, I've seen shy, introverted individuals grow into charismatic sales leaders. I've witnessed the pride in someone's eyes when it just 'clicks' for them - when they get that "aha! moment" of realizing they *can* do this. But, I want to be clear—this isn't a magic wand. It requires work, dedication, and a willingness to learn and grow, but if you're ready to put in the effort, if you're willing to trust the process and follow the blueprint, the results can be truly life-changing.

When I first started, it was pretty basic. I'd create exercises one at a time (sales process, what to say when you knock on a door, goal setting, etc.), and then I'd compile these into a three-ring binder—but it didn't stay that way for long.

The program quickly evolved into an online platform. Now, when they log in to the training – *BOOM!* There it is, every single detail of what we do at Cornerstone Construction (roofing, siding, gutters, windows, solar, etc.). We dive into product knowledge, warranties, and everything you could possibly need to know about our CRM. Next, we have the "Required Apps to Download." They click on the video for app number one, and it shows them step by step how to set up the account. App number two, same deal. It doesn't stop there— we teach them as much as we possibly can.

We've got a dozen-plus videos on lead generation techniques. We're talking about how they can go out and generate their own leads to hit their financial goals. We cover the sales process in-depth—how to go through it and actually close a deal. And there are many more sections on how to do their job, become a professional in this industry, and earn six figures.

Now, you might be thinking, *Hunter, why go through all this trouble? Why not just show them how to do it?*

Well, if you're serious about building a scalable business, you need to create a system that can run without you. Imagine this: Because you've got 95 percent of that stuff in video form, you never have to have the same conversation twice. It's like having a clone of myself that never gets tired, never loses patience, and is always available. That's right, no more being stuck in a truck or chained to a desk with a trainee.

Why should we waste our time showing every new hire how to download the three apps we use in our business? Why should I have to show them how to input a lead or create a contract, when I can put it into a video once and never have to say it again? That's valuable time we could be using to grow the company. This system only works if you hold people accountable.

Sometimes we'd have a rep come back and say, "Well, I don't know how to update this contract inside of the CRM."

My response, "You need to go back and watch *Six-Figure Blueprint* because we made a massive time investment into building out this training, and I expect you to use it and learn from it."

I'm not trying to be mean or rude here, but I expect them to be professionals, go all in, and learn it through that system—not ask me. It's about creating self-sufficient, proactive team members.

Once they've mastered the basics, we've got what we call the *Next Level Series*. This is where we take it up a notch. I go out and purchase content from industry titans, from top-notch trainers. I'm talking about courses on sales, lead generation, door-to-door techniques, etc., integrated into our platform, specifically for our sales reps.

Why go through the trouble of putting it on our platform instead of just sending them to the original course? It's not just about providing training—it's about creating a comprehensive, trackable system that ensures your team is constantly learning, growing, and improving.

If someone comes to us saying, "I'm struggling to hit my KPIs."

By having it on our platform, I can see exactly who's watching what, when they're watching it, and how they're progressing. In this way, I can look at their engagement with the *Next Level Series* and see if they're serious about their goals or if they're just doing the bare minimum to get by.

Now, the platform we used to build this is called Teachable, but there are plenty of softwares you can use, such as Kajabi and Thinkific. We landed on Teachable because it's really affordable and packs a punch with features. It's user-friendly, making it super simple to add videos and create a comprehensive course. It also allows you to add content review questions at the end of each video.

Here's what I do: I record the video, go back and watch it (yeah, I know, it's not always fun watching yourself), and then I add two or three questions for each video. For example, in the welcome section where I introduce myself, one of the questions is, "What's the name of my wife and son?" This isn't some narcissistic thing where I expect everyone to know my family tree. It's about cultivating a culture of attention to detail from day one.

We do this throughout the videos, testing them as they go. This way, we can see if they're really absorbing the material or just clicking through. It's like having a personal coach for each team member, making sure they're on track.

So, how do you actually build this out? It's simpler than you might think. Head over to teachable.com, sign up for an account, and create a new course. Go to the curriculum section, add a section, and name it. The best way to approach this is to create the framework first. Don't get stuck in your head thinking, *Oh, I don't know what to do. This is going to take forever. I need perfect videos.*

Listen, done is better than perfect.

Say it with me— *done* is better than *perfect.*

Why? Because this is a mindset that can revolutionize your business, and if you think you need to get it perfect right out of the gate, then you are just creating a recipe for never getting it done.

If you watch my videos, you'll see me sitting in front of a wall in our office, on my computer. These aren't Hollywood productions. They're not rehearsed; I'm not reading from a script. It's just real, authentic content. Heck, there are even videos where I burp and just keep going. Why? Because I want to show that I'm being authentic. It's just me and you, as a new team member, walking through the process together.

How to Build

Let's look at how you can approach building your own *Six-Figure Blueprint*. Start with the sections that cover all the basics here. We're talking:

1. Introduction
2. How to Schedule Your Week for Success
3. The Basics of the Job
4. Using the CRM
5. Product Knowledge
6. Lead Generation Techniques
7. Sales Process
8. Financing (if applicable)

Don't just stop at the big picture. Within each of these sections, you need to get granular. I'm talking about covering every single detail you can think of.

Your Introduction isn't just a "Hey, welcome aboard!" It's a deep dive into your company culture:

- Welcome to the company
- Our core values
- Our mission statement
- Our common mission

- Apps that need to be downloaded
- Any other crucial onboarding information

Your CRM section is not just going to say, "Here's our CRM." You're going to break it down:

- How to log in
- How to input a lead
- How to create a contract
- How to move a lead through different pipeline statuses

You're leaving no stone unturned here. The goal here is to think of every single question a new hire might have, and answer it before they even have time to ask. Remember, this is an evergreen project. It's always going to be evolving. Every time you finish a batch of videos, I guarantee in three weeks you'll think of more to add. And that's not just okay—it's ideal! That's how it should be. You should always be updating and improving.

The point is to get in there and create the framework. Set up your sections, fill them with videos. Don't let "perfect" be what keeps you from reaching "done."

When you access the resource, you'll see an example of how some of my sections are laid out.

Access The *Six-Figure Blueprint* Framework Example Here: TheRevolt.com/roadmap

Introduction

- ⚏ Welcome! **Start**
- ⚏ Our Mission **Start**
- ⚏ Our Promise To You **Start**
- <> More Than A Job. **Start**
- ⚏ Why Cornerstone? **Start**
- ⚏ Expectations **Start**
- <> S & S Personal Reviews **Start**
- ☰ Invite All Friends **Start**
- ⚏ Download Required Apps **Start**

Scheduled Success

- <> Your Schedule For Success **Start**
- ▶ Introduction (8:13) **Start**
- ▶ Vision (6:52) **Start**
- ▶ Planning (8:34) **Start**
- ▶ Weekly Routine (19:03) **Start**
- ▶ Performance Time (12:26) **Start**

Sales

- ⚏ Using the Contingency to Close **Start**
- ⚏ Sell VALUE! **Start**
- ⚏ SWIFT Sales System **Start**
- <> Overcoming Objections **Start**
- ⚏ Upgrades **Start**
- ⚏ Golden Pledge Warranty **Start**

Additional Tools

I highly recommend using loom.com. They offer free and cheap options that will allow you to create these videos easily and efficiently. Here's how it works:

1. Open Loom and hit record.
2. You can choose to screen record if you need to show something on your computer, or you can have yourself on video if that's more appropriate.
3. As soon as you start, you'll see a spot to put a title for the video. Make sure this matches whatever you have in Teachable for that section and video.
4. Once you're done recording, Loom will give you a link. Copy that link and paste it into Teachable. Boom—your video is now in your course.

Wait, we're not done yet. In Teachable, you're going to ask the questions we talked about earlier. This isn't just busywork—it's a way to ensure your team is actually absorbing the material. You can also upload documents, add text, whatever you need to make the lesson complete.

Here's an example of questions:

1 / 2

When was Cornerstone Construction started?

2016

2017

2018

2019

1 / 2

As we continue to grow we'll continue to...

Make money

Give

Open new markets

☲ **Download Required Apps**

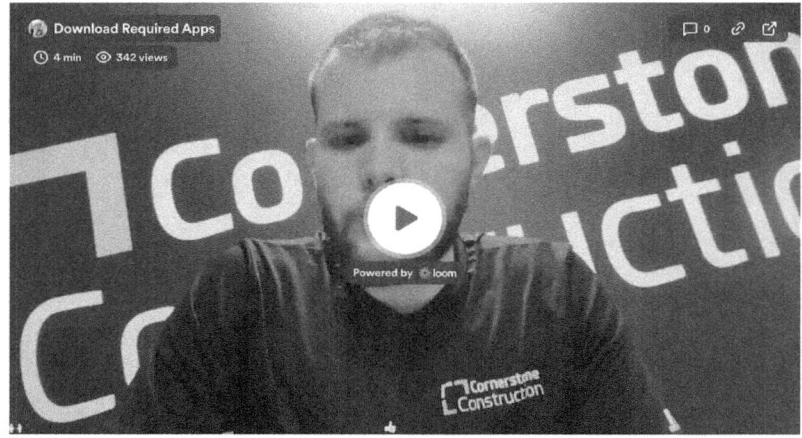

1 / 1

What are the required apps?

Outlook

Gmail

EagleView

iMeasure

Pitch Guage

Service Finance

Lead Scout App

HailTrace

RoofPRO

Acculynx - Field App

The beauty of this system is its simplicity. Sign up for Teachable, set up your sections, create your videos in Loom, upload them to Teachable, add your questions and any additional materials. That's it. You've just created a comprehensive training program that's going to save you hundreds of hours a year in babysitting team members.

Think about it—no more answering the same questions over and over. No more sitting down with every new hire to explain the basics. It's all there, ready to go, as soon as they join the team. The added bonus is that it creates consistency in your training. Every new hire gets the exact same information, presented in the exact same way, allowing you to set a standard for excellence from day one.

And don't forget—this is a living, breathing system that grows with your business that you can easily update as your business evolves.

Retention

This is where the rubber really meets the road in terms of developing and retaining top talent. We're not just talking about training here; we're talking about creating a comprehensive growth ecosystem that'll keep your team motivated, engaged, and constantly improving: growth tracks.

Growth tracks are about creating clear, tangible paths for advancement. If you've got salaried employees, you need to be crystal clear about how they can earn raises and bonuses. Let me give you an example from our playbook:

Once one of our reps hits $1 million in sales for the year—they get a $10,000 cash bonus, but we don't stop there. For every $500,000 in sales beyond that, they get an additional $10,000 bonus. So, let's say someone crushes it and sells $2.1 million in a year. Here's how that breaks down:

- $10,000 at $1 million
- Another $10,000 at $1.5 million
- And another $10,000 at $2 million

That's $30,000 in bonuses for the year. As you can imagine, that adds to motivation.

Here are some other pieces you can consider implementing:

1. Performance-Based Raises: Set clear metrics for salary increases. Maybe it's based on sales figures, customer satisfaction scores, or a combination of factors. The key is to make it transparent and achievable.
2. Profit Sharing: As your company grows, consider implementing a profit-sharing program. This aligns your team's interests with the company's success.
3. Title Advancement: Titles may seem like a small thing, but they matter to many. People want to see their growth reflected in their job title. Here are some examples:
- Sales Rep to Senior Sales Consultant
- Account Executive to Senior Account Executive
- Team Lead to Department Manager to Director

Each step up should come with increased responsibilities and increased compensation. This gives your team a clear ladder to climb.

The first two years in business, we didn't have a program or clear vision. When we got serious about building out the *Six-Figure Blueprint*, we weren't just creating a training program—we were casting a vision. We were showing our team what was possible, not just for the company but for them personally. In fact, a lot of people that came in when we started casting that vision are still with us today.

Here's how you can create that kind of vision for your business:

1. Regular Company Updates: Share the big picture regularly. Where's the company headed? What big goals are you working toward?
2. Individual Growth Plans: Work with each team member to create a personalized growth plan. Where do they want to be in one year? Five years? How can the company help them get there?
3. Mentorship Programs: Pair newer employees with seasoned veterans. This creates a culture of continuous learning and shows newer employees what's possible.
4. Success Stories: Regularly highlight team members who've grown within the company. Did someone start as a junior sales rep and work their way up to a director position? Shout it from the rooftops!
5. Clear Advancement Criteria: Don't make promotions a mystery. Clearly outline what it takes to move up in the company.

It's about crafting a narrative—a story that each of your team members can see themselves in. When someone joins your company, they should be able to envision not just their next year, but their next five or ten years. Better yet, when you do this right, you're not just creating a growth track—you're creating a legacy. You're building a company that people are proud to be a part of, a place where they can build their careers and their lives.

Remember, it's not just about the money or the title as standalone offerings. It's about creating a culture of growth and opportunity by investing in their growth, exposing them to new ideas, and showing them the bigger picture. That's why events and personal development opportunities are so crucial.

Personal Development

Financial incentives are just one piece of the puzzle. If you really want to develop and retain top talent, you need to invest in their personal development too. I'm talking about:

1. Bringing in Speakers: Get some heavy hitters to come in and share their wisdom. This shows your team that you're serious about their growth.
2. Personal Development Programs: Maybe it's a book club; maybe it's online courses. One of our Revolt members hosts a weekly "Lunch & Learn" with their team. The key is to keep them learning and growing.
3. Sending Them to Conferences: It's not just about what they learn; it's about the connections they make and the inspiration they get.

In our company, we send our people to RoofCON—the biggest conference in the roofing industry. Now, full disclosure, I'm the founder of this particular conference, but that's not why we send our team there. We send them because it's eye opening. We're talking over 5,000 roofers, hundreds of vendors, and speakers like Tim Tebow, John C. Maxwell, Ed Mylett, Tom Bilyeu, Jesse Itzler, and Craig Groeschel. Its main purpose isn't just to improve their knowledge of the industry. In fact, there's very little roofing-specific knowledge included. Instead, we're highly focused on developing individuals as leaders and leaving a legacy you're proud of. Attending a conference like that is like injecting pure motivation and knowledge directly into your people's veins.

Here are some of the personal results we get to see from our team members after they attend RoofCON that really gets me fired up:

- Getting clean or sober
- Achieving financial freedom
- Losing weight
- Saving their marriage
- Moving in to leadership positions within our company

These are the things that create loyalty and drive long-term success because these are the things that really matter to people.

So, what are the key elements of a successful leadership development program? Let me break it down for you:

1. Training: This is your foundation. You've got to give them the knowledge and skills they need to succeed.
2. Testing: Don't just assume they've absorbed the information. Test them. Make sure it's sticking.
3. Discussion: Talk through what they've learned. This helps with retention and gives you a chance to clear up any misunderstandings. This can be done with fellow reps through training.
4. Accountability: Hold them to high standards. Make sure they're putting what they've learned into practice.
5. Mentoring: Once they've mastered something, have them teach it to others. There's no better way to solidify knowledge than by teaching it.

This last point—mentoring—is where true leadership is born. When your team members start pouring into others, that's when you know you've created something special.

Building a successful eight-figure business is about creating a culture where people can grow, thrive, and reach their full potential. When you do that, the sales will take care of themselves. So, take a hard look at your development and incentive programs. Are they truly serving your team? Are they creating the kind of loyalty and motivation that'll take your business to the next level? If not, it's time to make some changes. Because at the end of the day, your business is only as strong as the people who make it run. Invest in them, and they'll invest in you. That's how you build a legacy that lasts.

Involving Your Team is Key

Creating growth tracks and opportunities isn't just about you sitting in your office and deciding what's best for your team. It's about collaborating with your team by getting them involved in the process. Remember, your team members are on the front lines every day. They have insights and ideas that you might never think of. So, here's what I want you to do. Sit down with your team and have open, honest conversations about what they want to see in terms of growth opportunities.

Ask them:

- What skills do you want to develop?
- What kind of leadership training would be most valuable to you?
- How do you envision your career path within the company?

It's not just about money. Sure, financial incentives are important, but don't stop there. Ask them how you can pour into them as leaders. Maybe it's mentorship programs or going to events. Perhaps it's giving them opportunities to lead projects or teams.

By involving your team in this process, you're not just creating better growth tracks—you're building buy-in. You're showing your team that their voice matters by valuing their input. And, believe me, that kind of engagement is priceless.

Now, as we wrap up this chapter on training and retaining talent, I want you to keep one thing in mind: Everything we've discussed here isn't just about making your current business better; it's about setting the stage for massive growth.

Next, we're going to take all the principles we've been talking about and apply them to a different area of your business – marketing. This means going back to *REYG*, knowing your numbers, and discussing the tools that will do the work for you.

Remember:

1. Continuous improvement is the lifeblood of any eight-figure business and crucial for retaining top talent.
2. Implement a comprehensive training program like the *Six-Figure Blueprint* to systematically onboard and develop your team.
3. Use platforms like Teachable to create an online training hub and tools like Loom for easy video creation.
4. Don't let perfection be the enemy of progress. Start building your training program now and improve it over time.
5. Create clear growth tracks with tangible paths for advancement, including performance-based raises, bonuses, and title progressions.
6. Invest in your team's personal development through speakers, conferences, and personal growth programs.
7. Involve your team in creating growth opportunities. Their input is valuable and builds buy-in for your development initiatives.

CHAPTER 8

Levers of Scale

O n this stop of the roadmap, we're going to turbocharge your marketing efforts, not just by talking about flashy ads or catchy slogans, but by diving deep into the nuts and bolts of what makes for successful marketing. We're going to explore techniques for setting marketing goals that align perfectly with your business objectives, and cover a wide range of topics, designed to give you a lever to pull that will scale your marketing efforts exponentially.

#1. Reverse Engineering Your Goals for Marketing Success

Remember how we talked about *REYG* (Reverse Engineering Your Goals) back in Chapter 5? Well, we're going to apply that same principle to your marketing efforts. But this time, we're drilling down to two crucial metrics: how many leads you need and your customer acquisition cost (CAC).

If you use the *Clarity Calculator* mentioned previously, you'll have a clear understanding of exactly how many leads, appointments, and contracts you need per month to hit your goals, but let's walk through an example to make this crystal clear:

- Your company's goal for the year: $1 million in sales
- Your average contract value: $4,000
- Contracts needed to achieve goal: 250
- Close rate: 50 percent
- Appointments needed to achieve contracts: 500
- Lead-to-appointment ratio: 50 percent
- Leads needed to achieve goal: 1,000

In other words: 1,000 leads → 500 appointments (50 percent conversion) → 250 contracts (50 percent close rate) → $2 million revenue.

So, your magic number is 1,000 leads. That's what you need to focus on generating.

You have to pay close attention to your CAC because you need to know how much you can afford to spend to acquire a customer based on your industry, your gross margin, and your net margin.

Also, know that whoever spends the most to acquire the customer will always win. Let that sink in for a moment.

If we're in the same market, competing against each other, and I'm willing to spend $1,000 to acquire a customer while you're only willing to spend $200, guess who's going to win? That's right– me.

"But doesn't that mean you're making less money?"

Not necessarily. I might be charging more, or maybe I'm willing to make less per customer, because I know I can sell more jobs than you.

For many service-based businesses, if you can keep your CAC under 5 percent of revenue, you're in a good spot. In my business, if I can keep my CAC at 5 percent, I'll pay for those leads over and over and over again until they stop sending them to me. It's that valuable.

Using a $10,000 average contract value as an example, that means I'm willing to spend $500 to acquire a customer. What do I mean by 'acquire'? I'm talking about spending that money on ads, on leads, on my agency to run the ads. When I average everything out, I'm spending $500 or less to acquire that one customer.

So, you need to understand two things:

1. What you want your customer acquisition costs to be.
2. What you can afford it to be.

If you are in an industry with higher margins, you may be able to afford 10 percent or even higher. You have to look at your margins and decide what that number is for your business.

Remember, this isn't just about crunching numbers. It's about creating a sustainable, scalable marketing strategy that aligns with your business goals. By reverse engineering your goals and understanding your CAC, you're setting yourself up for marketing success.

#2. Tracking Your Marketing Efforts: The Key to Unlocking Marketing Success

The second aspect of scaling your marketing: tracking.

"But we've got a CRM for that!"

I'm sure your CRM is great, but there's power in simplicity, and that's where our Lead Tracking Sheet comes in.

Access The Lead Tracking Sheet Here: TheRevolt.com/roadmap

Think of it like the Job Profitability Sheet we talked about earlier, but for your leads. We use Google Sheets for this, and I'll explain to you why it's so powerful.

Every single lead that we get goes into this sheet, allowing for all their data in one spot:

- The sales rep assigned to the lead
- Customer information
- Lead source (this is crucial, so pay attention)
- Status of the lead (bad lead, good lead, closed, not closed, in progress)
- Revenue (if the lead converts to a sale)

Now, why do we go to all this trouble? Because we want to attribute revenue to each lead source.

You see, you're not just going to have one overall CAC for your company. You're going to have a CAC for each lead source. This is because not all marketing channels are created equal. Some lead sources are going to perform better than others, and you need to know which ones are your winners and which ones are bleeding you dry. Let me give you an example.

Say we're running ads on both Facebook and Google AdWords. We track everything through our Lead Tracking Sheet, and here's what we find:

- Google AdWords: CAC of $300 per customer
- Facebook Ads: CAC of $800 per customer

Where do you think we're going to want to spend more money?

That's right, Google AdWords. We're acquiring customers for almost a third of the price compared to Facebook. Why would we spend nearly three times as much on Facebook when we can get better results from Google?

This is the power of tracking your lead sources and attributing revenue to them. It allows you to see what your CAC is for each marketing channel.

This data doesn't just tell you where to spend more—it tells you where you might need to optimize. Maybe your Facebook ads aren't performing well because your targeting is off, or your ad copy needs work. If you track this month over month, then this granular data will give you the insights you need to make those tweaks and improvements.

Also, this isn't static. Markets change. Consumer behavior shifts. What works today might not work as well tomorrow. By consistently tracking this data, you're able to spot trends and adjust your strategy in real time.

Here's another benefit—this data becomes invaluable when you're planning your marketing budget. Instead of guessing or going with your gut, you have hard numbers to back up your decisions. You can confidently allocate more budget to your high-performing channels and scale back on the ones that aren't delivering.

If we need 250 customers at $4,000 each to hit our goal of $1 million and each of those 250 customers cost us $300 through Google AdWords, we've spent $75,000 to acquire $1 million in business. This works out to 7.5 percent CAC.

To put it more simply, you are spending $300 for every $4,000 job you bring in. You should be able to look at your margins and make a quick decision to continue the marketing campaign or not for that lead source.

The Lead Tracking Sheet can be set up and maintained by a team member, or, like us, you can use a virtual assistant. This level of insight into your marketing performance is what allows you to make data-driven decisions that can dramatically improve your ROI.

Here's your action plan:

1. Set up your Lead Tracking Sheet (we'll provide the template).
2. Make sure every lead gets entered, without exception.
3. Regularly review your data (I recommend at least monthly, if not weekly).
4. Use this data to inform your marketing decisions.

Remember, understanding your customer acquisition costs—both overall and per lead source—is crucial. You can use those numbers to make smart, strategic decisions that will drive your business forward.

#3. *Seven-Figure Handshakes*: The Power of Strategic Networking

Now let's talk about one of the most powerful lead generation tactics you can use in your company, the *Seven-Figure Handshakes*—a straightforward, roll-up-your-sleeves kind of strategy that can yield incredible results.

At its core, *Seven-Figure Handshakes* is about creating your own networking group. We're going to give you this resource—a spreadsheet that's going to be your roadmap to building these powerful connections.

Access The *Seven-Figure Handshakes* Spreadsheet Here: TheRevolt. com/roadmap

You're going to identify one person from each trade in your area. We're talking plumbers, home inspectors, HVAC specialists, alarm system installers, solar panel experts, pest control professionals, etc. In fact, our spreadsheet has about forty-five different trades listed.

If you're thinking that it sounds like a lot of work, then you're right; it does take some effort, but the payoff is huge. Two of our best sales reps are introverts. They don't knock on doors, but they consistently sell seven figures a year for our company. How? By building these strategic relationships.

Here's the step-by-step strategy:

1. Use the spreadsheet. On the left, you'll see you've got all the trades listed. To the right, you're going to fill out the name, number, and email for each contact.
2. Head to social media. Facebook groups are a goldmine for this. Don't just post asking for recommendations. Instead, search for keywords like "plumber" or "pest control."

3. Look for existing recommendation threads. You'll find plenty of posts where people have asked, "Who's the best plumber in Brooklyn?" or "Need a great pest control guy in San Diego."

4. Reach out to the recommended professionals. Your message can be simple. "Hey, I'm starting a networking group. We're starting small, and I'd really like to have a [their profession] join." Be strategic and go after the professionals with the biggest friends list.

5. Fill the spots one by one. Remember, only one per trade. This exclusivity is part of what makes the group valuable.

6. As you get four to five people on board, they'll help you fill the other spots. Aim for at least twenty to thirty people in your group.

Now, let's talk logistics. If you have an office, offer it up as a meeting space. This eliminates costs for your sales reps. If not, find a restaurant or café that'll let you use their space for free or cheap. Offer to cover breakfast or lunch for the group.

For our team, we recommend meeting once or twice a month. We usually host morning meetings and provide Chick-fil-A breakfast. It's a small investment that pays off big time in relationship building.

Here's why this works so well:

1. Exclusivity: With only one professional per trade, everyone knows they're not competing within the group.

2. Mutual Benefit: Everyone in the group is looking for leads, so there's a strong incentive to share.

3. Trust: Over time, you build genuine relationships. These aren't just business contacts —they become partners in success.

4. Consistency: Regular meetings keep you top of mind for referrals.

5. Scalability: As your group grows, so does your network of potential leads.

The beauty of this system is that it compounds over time. The longer your group exists, the stronger the relationships become, and the more valuable the leads get.

Also, here's a pro tip: Don't just think about what these contacts can do for you. Always be on the lookout for how you can help them. Remember a lawyer who needs a good plumber? Refer them to your plumber contact. Your generosity will come back to you tenfold.

It's a simple concept, but don't underestimate its power. This strategy alone can help your sales reps drastically scale up their business and leads. It's about building a community of professionals who support each other. It's about creating a network that not only feeds your business but also helps you serve your customers better by having trusted professionals you can refer them to. It's about building relationships that can truly transform your business.

#4. Community Relations: A Little-Known Power Tool for Lead Generation

Here's another powerful technique that's become a staple in our lead generation strategy. This is specific to a department or individual within your company who is dedicated to building relationships in your community. That's it. No sales quotas, no pressure to close deals—just pure, unadulterated relationship building. We call this position Community Relations. We hired someone specifically for this role. This isn't a sales rep moonlighting as a community liaison.

How does this translate to leads? Well, let me break it down for you.

At Cornerstone Construction, our specialty is roofing, solar, siding, gutters, and windows. So, our Community Relations person focuses on building connections with people who interact with homeowners on a daily basis. We're talking:

1. Real estate agents
2. Insurance agents
3. Property managers

These folks are gold mines for potential leads. Who's the first to know when a roof needs replacing? The real estate agent who's trying to sell the house. Who gets the call when a storm damages a roof? The insurance agent. Who's constantly dealing with property maintenance issues? You guessed it—property managers.

Our Community Relations Specialist's job is to build genuine, lasting relationships with these professionals. They're not out there trying to sell anything. Instead, they're positioning our company as a trusted resource, showing up month after month to check in with each new connection we establish. They're the face of our brand in the community.

Here's how we structure the role:

1. Salary: We provide a base salary to ensure they're not stressed about making ends meet.
2. Commission: We offer a small percentage of any business that comes from their efforts. This incentivizes them to build quality relationships without the pressure of a full sales commission structure.
3. Company Car: We provide a wrapped vehicle. This serves two purposes—it's a perk for the employee, and it's mobile advertising for our business.

Why this strategy works so well:

1. Trust: By not pushing for sales, our Community Relations person builds genuine trust, becoming a valued resource, not a pushy salesperson.
2. Consistency: They're out there every day, being the face of our company. This constant presence keeps us top of mind.
3. Mutual Benefit: We're offering value to these professionals by becoming their trusted partner for all things related to exteriors.
4. Long-Term Relationships: Unlike a one-off sale, these relationships continue to yield leads year after year.
5. Community Presence: This strategy establishes us as a fixture in the community. That's invaluable for brand reputation.

Implementing a Community Relations strategy is about embedding your business into the fabric of your community, and building a network of professionals who become advocates for your brand. When hiring for this role, look for someone who's naturally outgoing and genuinely enjoys building relationships. Sales experience can be a plus, but it's not necessary. What's crucial is their ability to connect with people authentically.

#5. Social Media Marketing: Harnessing the Power of Digital Connections

When done right, social media can be a lead-generating powerhouse for your business.

1. Organic Posts: First things first, your organic presence matters. This is about consistently showing up on your social media platforms, particularly Facebook. Share updates about your business, behind-the-scenes looks, customer

testimonials, and helpful tips related to your industry. The key here is to be personal. People want to do business with people, not faceless corporations.

When Cornerstone was starting out, we leveraged social media heavily. We didn't just post about our services; we shared our journey, our challenges, and our victories. This personal touch helped us build a loyal following that eventually transformed into leads and sales.

2. Facebook Groups: Facebook groups are gold mines for lead generation. Here's how to make them work for you:
    a. Join relevant groups in your industry or local area.
    b. Provide value: answer questions, offer advice, and be helpful without being pushy.
    c. Create your own group. This is huge—we built a Facebook group that grew to over 100,000 members. How? By consistently providing value and engaging with our community. We didn't just talk about our services; we created a space for discussion, sharing, and community building.
3. Giveaways: People love free stuff. Use this to your advantage. Regular giveaways can boost engagement and keep your brand top of mind.

At Cornerstone, our motto was "The more we grow, the more we give." We lived this out through constant giveaways and by showing up in our community. It wasn't just about promoting our brand; it was about giving back to the community that supported us.

4. Facebook Ads: Paid advertising like Facebook's ad platform is incredibly powerful, especially for businesses with seasonal

peaks. For example: If you're in HVAC, ramp up your ads during summer heat waves or winter cold snaps. In roofing? Target areas that have just been hit by storms.

Tim Ferriss, author of *The 4-Hour Workweek* has used Facebook ads extensively. By targeting fans of similar authors and podcasts, Tim has been able to reach a highly relevant audience to promote his books, podcasts, and courses— reaching millions of people worldwide.

He also uses retargeting ads to engage people who have visited his website or interacted with his content before, ensuring they remain engaged with his brand. This strategy has helped him build a large and dedicated following, driving sales and downloads.

As shown with Tim Ferriss, the key with Facebook ads is precise targeting. Just boosting a post with no specific targeting is like burning money. Use Facebook's detailed targeting options to reach exactly the right audience at the right time. This is one area where it can be really helpful to hire a professional.

5. Video Content: Facebook's algorithm loves video. Create short, engaging videos about your services, customer testimonials, or quick tips related to your industry.

6. Facebook Live: Go live regularly. This could be Q&A sessions, live demonstrations, or behind-the-scenes looks at your business. Live videos often get more engagement and reach than regular posts.

7. Utilize Stories: These twenty-four-hour posts are great for sharing quick updates or time-sensitive offers.

8. Engage, Engage, Engage: Don't just post and ghost. Respond to comments, ask questions, and create polls to boost engagement.

9. Leverage User-Generated Content: Encourage customers to share their experiences and reshare this content on your page. It's authentic and builds trust. You can even offer gift cards and incentives to clients for doing this.

10. Create a Content Calendar: Plan your posts in advance to ensure consistency and cover all aspects of your business.

These next three are best when used by a professional. I don't recommend blowing through ad dollars on any ad platform if you don't know what you're doing. Instead, find an agency, hire a professional from somewhere like Upwork, or hire a full-time marketing director.

11. Use Facebook Pixel: This tool allows you to track conversions from Facebook ads, optimize ads based on collected data, and remarket to people who have already interacted with your website.

12. Experiment With Different Ad Formats: Try carousel ads, collection ads, and instant experience ads to see what resonates best with your audience.

13. Local Awareness Ads: If you're a local business, use Facebook's local awareness ads to target people in your specific area.

Remember, social media marketing is not about immediate sales. Don't just show up when you want something. Instead, focus on building relationships, providing value, and staying top of mind—consistently. When done right, it creates a community around your brand that naturally leads to more business and turns social media from a time-waster into a lead-generating machine.

#6. Door-to-Door Sales

Don't underestimate the power of good old-fashioned door-to-door sales. In an age of digital marketing, this traditional method can still be incredibly effective. Here's why:

1. Personal Touch: Nothing beats face-to-face interaction for building trust and rapport.
2. Immediate Feedback: You get instant reactions to your pitch, allowing you to refine your approach on the spot.
3. Targeted Approach: You can focus on specific neighborhoods or demographics.
4. Overcoming Digital Fatigue: In a world of online ads, a personal visit can stand out.

Tips for Effective Door-to-Door Sales:

- Train your team well. They're the face of your company.
- Respect people's time and space. Be polite and know when to walk away.
- Leave behind valuable information, even if they're not interested right now.
- Follow up. A second visit or call can often seal the deal.

#7. Google Products

Leveraging Google's suite of products can be a game-changer for your business.

Google Guaranteed and Local Service Ads (LSA): These are powerful tools for local businesses that provide a badge of trust and put you at the top of search results. The best part? You only pay when someone contacts you through the ad, and you can manage these yourself.

Google AdWords: Outside of your "busy" season, AdWords can keep the leads flowing. It allows for precise targeting and can be adjusted in real time based on performance.

Google Maps (The Snack Pack): This is crucial for local businesses. Optimize your Google My Business profile:

- Add high-quality photos.
- Encourage customer reviews.
- Keep your information up to date.
- Use relevant categories and attributes.

Brian Chesky, co-founder and CEO of Airbnb, utilized Google Ads and Google Maps to drive traffic and build visibility for Airbnb during its early stages. "We had to make sure people could find us online, and Google Ads was key to that strategy," Brian Chesky said.

In the early days, Chesky and his team used Google Ads to reach potential travelers searching for accommodations. By targeting relevant keywords, Airbnb was able to attract a steady stream of visitors to their website.

Additionally, integrating with Google Maps allowed Airbnb listings to show up in location-based searches, making it easier for users to find and book unique accommodations. This combination of Google Ads and Google Maps was instrumental in Airbnb's rapid growth and global reach.

#8. Bing Ads

Don't overlook Bing! While it might not have Google's market share, it's less competitive, which can mean lower costs per click. Plus, Bing users tend to be older and have higher income levels, which could be perfect for certain businesses.

My personal thoughts on SEO (search engine optimization): While SEO isn't dead, its effectiveness has diminished because of the prominence of paid ads and map results. Organic results are often pushed far down the page. While you shouldn't ignore SEO completely, be cautious about investing too heavily in it. Focus on a balanced approach that includes paid ads, local optimization, and organic SEO.

When it comes to marketing, what you measure is what you can improve. Here are the most critical metrics you need to keep an eye on:

1. Lead Cost: This is your total ad spend divided by the number of leads generated.
2. Customer Acquisition Cost (CAC): We've talked about this before, but it's worth repeating. This is the total cost to acquire a paying customer.
3. Return on Investment (ROI): This tells you how much revenue you're generating for every dollar spent on marketing.

These metrics are your guiding light. They tell you which marketing channels are working and which ones are bleeding you dry.

Pulling the Right Levers

Now, when it comes to accelerating marketing effectiveness, it's all about pulling the right levers. Those levers are going to be different for every business. In the contracting space, for instance, I often see Google AdWords outperforming Facebook ads, but that might not be true for your business. Maybe you're killing it with door-to-door sales or referrals, or maybe email campaigns to past customers are your golden ticket. The point is, you need to test, measure, and optimize based on your unique situation.

Identifying Your Best Lead Sources

This is where that Lead Tracking Sheet we talked about earlier comes in handy. By attributing revenue to each lead source, you can clearly see which ones are giving you the highest return.

You're probably thinking that you don't have time for all these spreadsheets and all this tracking. I hear you. That's why I recommend considering a virtual assistant to help with this kind of data entry and analysis.

There are services out there that can connect you with affordable VAs and help you manage them. We currently have ten-plus VAs working for us full-time, and are learning how we can utilize them even more.

Find The Virtual Assistant Agency I Use Here: TheRevolt.com/ roadmap

When to Cut Your Losses

Here's a question I get a lot, "Once I've determined my target CAC, how long do I let a lead source run if it's not hitting that target?"

The answer? It depends. Let's say your target CAC is 5 percent of revenue. You might be willing to let it creep up to 7 percent before you pull the plug. If it goes beyond that, you've got to make a business decision.

Now, if you're struggling for business and need the cash flow, you might let it go a bit higher out of necessity. But be careful—if it eats too far into your margin, you're just digging yourself into a hole.

Remember, these decisions aren't set in stone. You've got to be flexible and adapt based on your current situation. If you're flush with business, you can afford to be pickier about your CAC. If times are lean, you might need to loosen those standards a bit. The key is to always be aware of your numbers. Let's talk about Brian Chesky and Airbnb again. In an interview with Reid Hoffman on the *Masters of Scale* podcast, Chesky shared, "We were really focused on unit economics from the beginning. We asked, 'Can we make money on every single transaction?' And more importantly, 'How quickly can we pay back our customer acquisition cost?'"

In regard to Airbnb's early days, Chesky revealed, "We realized that if we could get a customer to return and book again, our CAC would effectively be cut in half. This insight led us to shift our focus from just acquiring new customers to ensuring our existing customers had an amazing experience and would come back. We even made the controversial decision to spend more on customer service than on marketing in our early years. This focus on retention and repeat bookings, driven by our understanding of CAC, was a key factor in our growth."

In the world of eight-figure businesses, these kinds of data-driven decisions are what separate the winners from the losers. It's not about gut feelings or hunches. It's about cold, hard numbers.

So, get intimate with your metrics. Don't just set it and forget it. Use that Lead Tracking Sheet, regularly review your metrics, and be ready to make tough decisions based on what the data is telling you. Don't be afraid to cut underperforming channels, even if they're your personal favorites. Make decisions based on the data, not emotions. And always, always be testing and optimizing. It's a constant process of measurement, analysis, and adjustment. But when you get it right, when you find those high-performing channels and optimize them, that's when you'll really reap the benefits.

We've covered a lot of ground in this chapter. We dove deep into the levers of scale for your marketing efforts, from reverse engineering your goals to leveraging various marketing channels. We talked about the importance of tracking your metrics, especially that all-important customer acquisition cost. Remember, what gets measured gets managed.

All the leads in the world won't mean a thing if you can't close them. That's why our next chapter is going to be all about mastering sales. Just like we've done with marketing, we'll be looking at sales through the lens of scalability. Because in the journey to eight figures and beyond, it's not just about making more sales—it's about creating systems that can consistently deliver results as your business grows.

So, take some time to digest what we've covered about marketing. Start implementing the tracking sheet, analyzing your data, and making those tough decisions about where to allocate your resources. Because when we continue along the roadmap to our stop at sales, you'll want to have a clear picture of where your leads are coming from and what they're costing you.

Remember:

1. Use *REYG* (Reverse Engineer Your Goals) to determine how many leads you need and your target customer acquisition cost (CAC).
2. Implement a comprehensive lead tracking system to attribute revenue to each lead source and optimize your marketing spend.
3. The person who can spend the most to acquire a customer while maintaining profitability will often win in the market.
4. Leverage strategic networking through *Seven-Figure Handshakes* to create a powerful referral network across various trades.
5. Consider hiring a dedicated Community Relations Specialist to build lasting relationships with key professionals in your community.
6. Harness the power of social media marketing through organic posts, Facebook groups, targeted ads, and engaging content.
7. Don't overlook traditional methods like door-to-door sales, which can still be highly effective when done right.
8. Regularly analyze your marketing metrics (lead cost, CAC, ROI), and be prepared to cut underperforming channels based on data, not emotions.

CHAPTER 9

Mastering Sales

In this chapter, we're diving deep into the art and science of sales. Our focus? Developing a sales system and process that makes it easy for your reps to close deals. This isn't about reinventing the wheel every time—it's about creating a repeatable, scalable process that your entire team can follow.

From the initial contact to the final handshake, you'll have the techniques you need to build a blueprint for sales success. Also, with examples from sales trainers who have proven sales processes, you'll also be able to tailor what you learn in this book to your business.

A great process is only as good as the people executing it. That's why we're going to dive into accountability and training for your sales reps. Remember the *Six-Figure Blueprint* we discussed earlier? We're going to build on that, showing you how to implement it effectively and use it to turn your sales team into a group of high-performing professionals. So, make room in your toolbox because you're not just going to learn about how to manage your sales team, but how to lead them to unprecedented success.

Simplicity is the Ultimate Sophistication in Sales

Back in July 2018, I was hired to train a company's sales team for a month. While I was there, I didn't just teach—I put my money where my mouth was and went out selling myself. The result? Eighty-two jobs closed, over a million dollars in sales, all in one month.

How did I do it? With a simple process that I could walk a homeowner through in less than fifteen minutes. This experience hammered home a crucial truth: In sales, simplicity wins.

Here's what most homeowners are really looking at when choosing who to work with:

1. The product
2. The company
3. Most importantly, you (or your sales rep)

They're asking themselves, "Is this person trustworthy? Can they do the job right?"

This brings me to a huge takeaway that every business owner needs to understand: ***Our job is to make our sales reps' jobs as easy as possible***. We want to maximize their close ratio because when they win, we win. How do we do that? By giving them a clear, simple process to follow.

Why is this so crucial? Because your sales team is the engine that drives your revenue. The easier you make their job, the more deals they'll close, and the faster your business will grow.

Let's break this down:

1. Maximize Win Rate: Your goal should be to give your sales team the highest possible close rate. Every percentage point increase in their close rate translates directly to your bottom line.

2. Provide a Clear Process: A clear, repeatable sales process is like giving your team a roadmap to success. It takes the guesswork out of selling and allows your reps to focus on what matters: connecting with the customer.

Sales Processes

I mentioned my own simple process, but let's look at the Be REAL method by Ken Younce.

Ken explains the whole process perfectly. "Over my successful sales career, people often asked, 'What are you doing differently?' My answer was simple, 'I'm just being real.'

"While my passion for coaching and helping others was strong, I realized that simply telling people to 'be real' wasn't enough. I needed a structured system, which led to the development of my Be REAL sales methodology.

"Be REAL is both a literal approach to sales and an acronym that defines the core values of the methodology it adopts.

"**Relate:** Build rapport by finding common ground with the client. For instance, if they mention a hobby or interest, engage in a related conversation to establish trust.

"**Educate:** Position yourself as an expert by providing valuable information. For example, share insights that highlight your expertise.

"**Ask:** Ask the right questions at the right times to move the process along effectively. Questions should uncover needs and preferences, like 'What are your main concerns with your current provider?'

"**Listen:** Practice active listening to understand the client's needs fully. It is crucial to success. You should reflect back what they say to confirm understanding and show empathy."

Core Principles of Be REAL:

- **Relationships Over Sales**: Never set out to make a sale. Set out to build a relationship. Relational sales will always produce much more long-term value than short-term transactional sales ever will. Referrals, reviews, upsells, repeat business—all will be normal results of relational sales.
- **Conversations Over Pitches**: People have been pitched to death! Pitches, no matter how good, do not humanize clients. They make them a number, which hinders our ability to make them feel valued. That is no way to start a relationship.
- **Journey Over Destination**: A roofing D2D legend, Ben Menchaca, coined the phrase, "Love the process, not the results." This phrase directly parallels the Journey Over Destination principle. We cannot be intentional (and in essence, effective) within each portion of the sales

process (Journey) if we are only focusing on the result (Destination).

- **Win the Moment**: If you focus on only one version of a 'win'—a closed deal today—you will, more often than not, miss the value of small wins you can pull from every opportunity. Things like future appointments, referrals, reviews, insight, and experience are all small wins you can gain outside of a signed deal. As Myron Golden said, "All work works. It either works 'for' you, or it works 'on' you."

Younce sums up Be REAL by saying, "The benefits of the Be REAL approach are immeasurable in any industry and market. True sales success stems from self-confidence and authenticity, not memorized scripts or stock responses; it's simply not authentic! Clients can easily detect insincerity and prefer real conversations with real people. Embrace comfortable conversations that foster valuable relationships, and you will separate yourself from the pack!"

The Home Doctor TECHNIQUE

And now let's look at The Home Doctor TECHNIQUE by Noah Williams.

Here's how Noah explains his technique: "Scaling a business to eight figures requires not just an innovative product or service but also a highly effective sales process. One such process, designed to handle homeowner objections and convert leads into committed clients, is The Home Doctor TECHNIQUE. This method offers a structured, step-by-step approach by following the TECHNIQUE.

"**T**rust Building.

"**E**xploring Property.

"**C**ondition Assessment.

"**H**istory and Heritage.

"**N**arrate Install Expectations.

"**I**llustrate Remedies.

"**Q**uestion for Commitment.

"**U**nderstanding Price, Payments, and Pain Points.

"**E**asy Paperwork."

Trust Building

The foundation of The Home Doctor TECHNIQUE is trust. Without trust, no homeowner will feel comfortable moving forward with a significant project. The first step, **Trust Building**, involves creating a genuine connection with the homeowner.

Start by observing the home for personal items that you can relate to. For instance, family photos, sports memorabilia, or a fancy car in the driveway can all provide natural conversation starters. Talking about these with the homeowner will allow you to naturally form trust with the homeowner.

Engage the homeowner in discussions about their personal interests. The more you get them talking, the more they will begin to trust you. Remember to involve all decision-makers present in the home. If you see a spouse or partner, make sure to include them in the conversation to build trust with *both* parties.

At the end of this phase, ask Three Crucial Discovery Questions to "discover" the homeowner's objections or "pain points" *before* we get too far into the appointment:

1. **How long have you been thinking about replacing your roof?** This question helps gauge the urgency and decision-making timeline.
2. **How soon are you looking to start a project like this?** This question uncovers any immediate plans or financial preparations.
3. **Would there be anything stopping you from starting the project today?** This question will more than likely get the homeowner to tell you *exactly* why they wouldn't want to make a decision on the spot. We *only* need to ask this *if* we were not able to discover the pain points by asking the previous discovery questions. If a homeowner is getting other estimates, or if they don't like making same-day decisions, we want to pull out those pain points *before* we try to ask them for the deal.

Knowing the customer's pain points will allow us to know what the homeowner's objections are to moving forward with the project, which will allow us to correctly diagnose and handle their objections in History and Heritage.

Explore the Property

Once trust is established, and pain points are discovered, move on to **Explore the Property**. This step is about learning more about the specific issues the homeowner wants to address. Ask the homeowner to show you problem areas, like the leaky roof or damaged flooring. Use this opportunity to demonstrate your expertise by using industry-specific terms such as hat vents, intake ventilation, subflooring, and baseboard trim.

As you explore, continue building trust by showing genuine interest in the homeowner's concerns. Take notes and listen attentively to their descriptions of the problems. This not only helps in diagnosing the issue accurately but also reinforces your professionalism and reliability.

Next, we will incentivize the homeowner to watch the test case videos, by offering $100 off for each video they watch. The test cases are testimonial videos of our past customers that have been put together into a funnel and categorized by the type of pain point/objection that was discovered in Step 3. Typically you will create multiple sheets, with their own funnels, to 'profile' and categorize your test cases based on job type, customer pain points, and miscellaneous details about the customers (dog lovers, car lovers, hail-damage customers, customers looking for a cheap job, etc.).

These funnels are accessed by the homeowner scanning a QR Code that will take them to the testimonial videos most relevant to their situation. For instance, if a homeowner has an objection or pain point of "other estimates," we are going to give them the test cases of our previous homeowners that had that same pain point before they chose to work with us. This helps to naturally take away the objections of prospective clients.

Condition Assessment

The **Condition Assessment** step involves a thorough evaluation of the homeowner's problems. Use advanced tools like thermal imagers, moisture meters, and digital microscopes to conduct a comprehensive inspection video, known as the Digital Exam. The goal is to build a sense of urgency by clearly identifying and documenting the issues.

Adopt the WORK formula for the Digital Exam:

- **W**alk up to the problem.
- **O**bserve the conditions.
- **R**isk factors.
- **K**eep the video under two minutes.

This approach ensures you present a concise yet detailed assessment, making it clear why immediate action is necessary. By highlighting risk factors and potential consequences, you can help homeowners understand the importance of resolving their issues promptly.

In this step, you will also be creating the remedies, and coming up with the pricing for their project. We want to make sure pricing is prepared *before* we go back into the home and start to go through our presentations. Typically, you will be creating "good, better, and best" pricing, to give the homeowner multiple options for their repairs.

History and Heritage

Next is **History and Heritage**, where you present your company's background and unique selling points. This step is crucial for differentiating your business from competitors. Identify three unique aspects of your company—such as exceptional communication, strong family values, or a solid track record—and weave these into your company's history.

Share stories about the company's origins, milestones, and successes to make the presentation relatable and engaging. Use industry reports, like the cost versus value report, to price condition the homeowner. For example, compare the cost of a high-quality roof to buying a luxury car, emphasizing that superior products and services come with a higher price tag but offer greater value and reliability.

Narrate Install Expectations

In the **Narrate Install Expectations** step, show the homeowner what to expect during the installation process. Create detailed videos where you outline each component of the project, from start to finish, and narrate an explanation for each step. This ensures the homeowner understands the process and timeline.

Consider making multiple videos for different project types—such as tile roofing, shingle roofing, metal roofing, and flat roofing—since each has unique procedures. A well-narrated install expectation video reassures the homeowner that you know what you're doing and sets clear, accurate expectations.

Illustrate Remedies

Illustrating Remedies involves presenting specific solutions to the homeowner's problems. So, prepare a remedy kit that includes all the components you plan to use, explain the benefits and logistics of each component, and let the homeowner physically examine them.

Follow the ILL formula:

- **I**nclude all components.
- **L**ogistics of components.
- **L**et them touch it.

This hands-on approach helps homeowners appreciate the quality of the materials and understand why they are necessary. Tailor your pitch to address specific diagnoses, ensuring that each remedy is relevant to the homeowner's issues.

Question for Commitment

The **Question for Commitment** step is about confirming the homeowner's readiness to proceed. Ask, "Past price or payment, would there be any reason we couldn't get your project started today?" This question aims to uncover any remaining objections before discussing pricing.

Listen carefully to their response. If they express concerns or hesitations, address them directly. This step ensures that you have identified and alleviated all objections, making the homeowner more likely to commit to the project.

Understand Price and Payments

In **Understanding Price and Payments**, present your pricing and payment options clearly. Offer three packages—good, better, and best—to provide choices that cater to different needs and budgets. Highlight the middle option as the most balanced choice.

Break down the costs into small, manageable numbers. For example, present $4,399 as simply $4,399, and show payment options with small monthly amounts. Then apply any test case discounts based on the videos the homeowner watched, making the final price more appealing.

Easy Paperwork

Finally, make the **Easy Paperwork** step as seamless as possible. Prepare all necessary documents in advance, including credit applications and contingency filings. The goal is to streamline the process, making it quick and hassle-free for the homeowner.

Set the stage for a five-star review by explaining your commitment to delivering an exceptional experience. Before leaving, ask this concluding question, "What made you decide to move forward with me today?" This reinforces their decision and reduces the risk of cancellations.

In conclusion, The Home Doctor TECHNIQUE provides a structured, step-by-step approach to sales that can significantly enhance your business's efficiency and customer satisfaction. By building trust, thoroughly assessing conditions, presenting tailored remedies, and handling objections systematically, you can convert more leads into committed clients. Implementing this technique not only helps address homeowner concerns effectively but also sets your business apart from competitors, paving the way for substantial growth and success in reaching eight figures.

Here are a few other sales processes to explore:

- **LAER**: **L**isten, **A**cknowledge, **E**xplore, **R**espond.
- **SNAP**: Keep it **S**imple, be i**N**valuable, **A**lign, raise **P**riorities.

The first sales process I ever created, SWIFT:

- **SWIFT**: **S**ell yourself, **W**ithdraw the problem, **I**nitiate confidence and expertise, **F**ocus on the pain, **T**alk timeline and pricing.

Each of these processes has its merits, but here's the key: It's not so much about which process you choose but how consistently you implement it. You can use an existing process or create your own, but consistency is king.

When you choose a sales process for your team, it's crucial that you enforce it religiously. Every sales rep should be following the same steps, in the same order, every single time. Why?

Because consistency allows for:

1. Easier Training: When everyone's following the same process, it's much easier to onboard new reps and coach existing ones.
2. Better Measurement: A consistent process gives you a baseline to measure against. You can more easily identify where in the process reps are struggling and provide targeted support.
3. Continuous Improvement: When everyone's doing the same thing, it's easier to spot what's working and what's not. You can then refine the process and see improvements across your entire team.
4. Scalability: As your business grows, a consistent sales process makes it easier to maintain quality across a larger team.

Tony Robbins, renowned life coach and business strategist, often says, "Success leaves clues." In sales, this means studying and replicating what works.

Robbins emphasizes the importance of understanding human psychology in sales. He says, "To effectively sell, you need to understand what people want and why they want it." By understanding the customer's needs and desires, a good sales rep can position themselves as the solution.

Robbins also touches on confidence in sales. He once said, "The only thing that's keeping you from getting what you want is the story you keep telling yourself." This underscores why it's so crucial to equip your sales team with a solid process and the right tools—it builds their confidence, which in turn makes them more effective.

Another great person to look at in sales is Grant Cardone. He famously said, "Success is no different than any other skill. Duplicate the actions and mindsets of successful people, and you will create success for yourself." This makes him a strong advocate for systematic approaches in sales.

Cardone emphasizes the importance of persistence and follow-up in sales. He's known for his 10X Rule, which essentially means putting in ten times more effort than you think you need to. In the context of our sales process, this could mean ensuring your team is diligent about following up with leads and not giving up after the first "no."

Cardone also stresses the importance of continuous improvement. He says, "There is no shortage of money on this planet, only a shortage of people thinking big enough." This aligns with our emphasis on recording sales pitches and continuously refining the process.

Practical Steps to Empower Your Sales Team

Now, let's talk practical steps to make your sales reps' jobs easier:

1. Implement a Consistent Sales Process: As we've discussed, having a clear, repeatable process is crucial.

   Have them record themselves so you can listen back to the recording and make critiques where necessary. Make sure they have a clear understanding of the process and help them improve.

2. Create a Compelling Sales Presentation: Develop a slideshow that guides your reps through each step of the sales process. This ensures they hit all the key points consistently.
   Have them bring an iPad or computer to the appointment, so they can walk the customer through the presentation.

Every step of your process is within that slideshow so no points are missed.

3. Use Preemptive Objection Handling: We've had great success with what we call our "Why Cornerstone" video.

Access "Why Cornerstone" Video Here: TheRevolt.com/roadmap

Bringing an iPad to appointments and showing the customer our "Why Cornerstone" video has been a game-changer.

Here's what we cover in the video:

1. Price concerns
2. Quality assurance
3. Company reputation
4. Awards and accolades
5. Qualifications and certifications
6. Manufacturer partnerships
7. Licensing and insurance
8. Community involvement

Essentially, we're anticipating and answering every question a homeowner might have about working with us before they have an opportunity to throw objections at our sales rep—giving our reps a higher close rate.

The Evolution of the Video

Our first "Why Cornerstone" video was a concise four to five minutes long. Our current version runs about ten minutes. Now, I'll be honest— when we first created the longer version, I was concerned it might be too much, but I've discovered after years of testing what we call "Video Sales Letters," that the lead becomes more qualified the longer they watch.

Why? Because someone who's willing to invest ten minutes of their time to watch a video about your company is already demonstrating a high level of interest. They're not just tire-kicking; they've already committed their time to learn more about you, which means they're genuinely considering doing business with you.

The Viewing Process

We've integrated this video seamlessly into our sales process. Here's how it works:

1. The sales rep arrives at the home to inspect the property.
2. Before starting, they hand the homeowner an iPad with the video loaded.
3. They simply ask, "While I'm inspecting your property, would you mind watching this video? It'll answer any questions you might have about Cornerstone, and when I get back, I'll be happy to address any additional questions too."

This approach is effective for several reasons:

- It makes productive use of the time the rep spends inspecting the property.
- It allows the homeowner time to absorb information at their own pace.
- It ensures consistency in how our company is presented.

Content of the Video

In the video, I personally address the main concerns homeowners typically have. We don't just tell; we show.

- We display thousands of testimonials.
- We flash reviews from Google and Facebook.

- We showcase our completed projects.
- We include video testimonials from satisfied homeowners.
- We highlight our community involvement and charitable work.

The goal is to create a comprehensive picture of who we are as a company and why homeowners should trust us with their project.

Looking at Grant Cardone's process when it comes to using video, he's all about that high-energy, in-your-face approach. He's kicking off sales presentations with these amped-up intro videos (which can be pre-recorded and automated, as we'll get into shortly), peppering in customer testimonials like confetti, and even insisting on video calls when in-person interactions aren't possible. He advocates for your sales team to share their screens and walk prospects through slick presentations that highlight your value and crush objections.

The Results

When the sales rep returns from the inspection and takes back the iPad, they ask a simple question, "Do you have any questions about the company at this point?"

More often than not, the answer is no. We've already addressed everything they might want to know.

This approach offers several advantages:

1. It establishes our legitimacy and credibility up front.
2. It showcases our product quality.
3. It demonstrates our commitment to the community.
4. It frees up the sales rep to focus on the specifics of the homeowner's project rather than selling the company.

The sales rep's job becomes much easier. As long as they conduct themselves professionally and address the specific needs of the homeowner, they should be able to close the sale. Their win rate should be significantly higher because we've already done much of the heavy lifting in terms of building trust and credibility.

Of course, there will always be some customers who are solely focused on getting the lowest price possible, but when the vast majority of homeowners are looking for a balance of quality, reliability, and value, this approach sets us up for success.

Implementing Your Own Version

If you're considering creating a similar video for your business, here are some tips:

1. Be comprehensive: Cover all possible objections and questions.
2. Use visual evidence: Include testimonials, reviews, and project photos.
3. Keep it engaging: Use a mix of speaking footage, graphics, and customer testimonials to maintain interest.
4. In this case, I'd go for a professional look. Even if you record footage yourself, have a professional put the video together with A Roll, B Roll, and background music to bridge and create smooth transitions throughout.

Remember, the goal of this video is to make your sales reps' jobs easier by doing much of the trust-building and credibility-establishing up front. It's an investment in your sales process that can pay dividends in higher close rates and more efficient sales calls.

By implementing a tool like the "Why Cornerstone" video, you're not just improving your sales process—you're demonstrating to potential customers that you value their time and want them to have all the information they need to make an informed decision.

Educating the Homeowner: The Core of the Sales Process

When our sales rep returns from inspecting the property, their primary role shifts to that of an educator. This is crucial because an informed customer is more likely to make a decision they feel confident about. Here's how this education process unfolds:

1. Assessment Breakdown:
   - The rep doesn't just say, "You need a new XYZ"; they explain why.
   - They use photos or videos taken during the inspection to illustrate issues.
   - They translate technical terms into language the homeowner can understand.
   - They explain the consequences of not addressing the issues they've found.
2. Product Education:
   - This isn't just about listing features. It's about explaining the benefits.
   - They might compare our materials to cheaper alternatives, explaining the long-term value.
   - They could use samples to let the homeowner see and feel the quality.
   - They explain how our product solves the specific issues found on the homeowner's roof.
3. Timeline and Pricing:
   - They provide a detailed project timeline, explaining each phase.
   - They offer various pricing options, explaining the differences in detail.
   - They might use a cost-benefit analysis to show the long-term savings of choosing quality.

Leveraging Your CRM to Supercharge Your Sales Process

Your CRM isn't just about keeping track of leads; it's about creating a seamless, automated system that works tirelessly to convert prospects into customers.

Before your sales rep even sets foot on a property, your CRM should be hard at work. We're talking about sending out strategic text messages and videos that start building credibility right from the get-go. You can even tailor these pre-visit communications to address specific objections.

Imagine this: You've got a library of video testimonials from satisfied customers, each addressing a common concern. One homeowner might say, "When we were looking for a contractor, we were really worried about the quality of the work." Another might chime in with, "We were concerned about the price, but . . ." You get the idea. The beauty of this approach is that you're proactively addressing objections before your sales rep even arrives. It's like sending out a team of happy customers to pave the way for your sales pitch.

You can divvy up these testimonials and send them out strategically. If you know a potential customer is particularly price-sensitive, you can make sure they see testimonials that address value for money. It's like having a crystal ball that lets you predict and solve your customer's concerns before they even voice them.

The momentum doesn't stop when your sales rep leaves the property. That's when your CRM really kicks into high gear. You can set up automated follow-ups that keep the conversation going. I've heard it said for years that the average sale takes seven follow-ups. We're talking videos, texts, emails—all working in harmony to nudge that prospect toward a "yes." And the best part? Your sales rep doesn't have to lift a finger. The CRM is doing all the heavy lifting. In the rare case that your CRM doesn't have automation capabilities, you can use a tool like RepCard.com that acts as a digital business card, funnel builder, canvassing tool, follow-up tool, competition board, and more.

Even after the job is done, you can automatically request reviews, suggest complementary services for cross-selling, and even ask for referrals. It's like having a tireless sales assistant that never sleeps, never takes a day off, and never misses an opportunity to grow your business.

Crafting Your Presentation

Now, you might be wondering, *How do I create a professional-looking presentation?* Don't worry, I've got you covered. There are several user-friendly platforms that can help you create stunning presentations, even if you're not a tech whiz.

1. Canva.com:
    - Free to use with a basic account.
    - Offers a premium account for advanced features.
    - User-friendly interface with drag-and-drop functionality.
    - Wide range of templates and design elements.
2. Ingage:
    - Specifically designed for sales presentations.
    - Allows for interactive elements.
    - Provides detailed analytics on user engagement.

The Power of Analytics

Speaking of analytics, this is where Ingage really shines. It offers in-depth tracking capabilities that can revolutionize your sales approach:

- Click Tracking: See exactly where prospects are engaging with your presentation.
- Rep Performance: Compare the performance of different sales reps.
- Funnel Analysis: Identify which sales funnels are most effective.
- Optimization Opportunities: Pinpoint areas where underperforming reps might need additional training or support.

By leveraging these insights, you can continually refine your sales process, coach your team more effectively, and ultimately, close more deals.

For smaller teams, Canva offers a free, user-friendly option to create slideshows. These can guide your sales reps through the entire sales process with homeowners, covering everything from introductions to warranties. This ensures consistency while aligning with your established sales approach.

Balancing Rewards and Consequences in Sales Performance Management

As we've previously discussed when talking about KPIs and accountability, it's crucial to have a well-rounded system that includes both rewards for good performance and consequences for underperformance. Let's dive deeper into this concept and explore how to implement it effectively in your sales team.

The Carrot: Rewarding Success

Recognizing and rewarding your top performers is essential for maintaining motivation and driving continued success. Here are some ways to incentivize your sales team:

1. Bonuses: financial incentives tied to performance metrics.
2. Growth Track: clear path for career advancement within the company.
3. Experiential Rewards: tickets to concerts, sporting events, or other experiences.
4. Competitions and Challenges: foster healthy competition among team members.

Remember, the key is to offer a mix of rewards that appeal to different motivations and personalities within your team.

The Stick: Implementing Consequences

While it's important to celebrate success, it's equally crucial to have consequences for underperformance. This ensures that everyone on the team is consistently striving for excellence. Here's how some companies approach this:

Some people will cut the bottom 20 percent of their sales team once a year. No matter what they're at, they'll cut the bottom 20 percent to make sure people are pushing to be at the top.

While this approach can be effective in maintaining a high-performing team, it's not the only way. Personally, I prefer a more personal approach that focuses on clear expectations and personalized goals.

Setting Clear Expectations

At Cornerstone, we use a tiered goal system:

1. The Minimum: $65,000 a month in sales. If they're not selling at least $65,000 a month in sales, it's no bueno. That's the minimum.
2. The Target: based on the individual's aspirations, but always above the minimum.
3. The Stretch: an ambitious target to push top performers.

Like we talked about in Chapter 3, the goal and the stretch goal should be based on what their goals are. Obviously, it should be greater than $65,000 because that's just the minimum, and we don't want any of our sales reps being average.

Quarterly Performance Review

We use a quarterly consequence system to allow for short-term fluctuations while maintaining accountability:

So, if they miss a goal for their quarter—let's say they may miss a month or two months or something like that—that's okay. I'm not going to get upset at them over that. But over the course of the quarter, they need to make up the difference.

For example:

- Month 1: $60,000 (missed by $5,000)
- Month 2: $50,000 (missed by $15,000)
- Month 3: needs to sell $85,000 to make up the $20,000 deficit

This system allows for flexibility while ensuring that the average monthly sales meet the minimum requirement over the quarter.

If a sales rep consistently underperforms, we have a structured approach to consequences:

1. Grace Period: for long-term, previously successful employees.
2. Written Warning: formal documentation of the performance issue.
3. Escalating Consequences: could include loss of salary, commission, or company vehicle.
4. Termination: as a last resort if performance doesn't improve.

You have to decide what this looks like for your business, but there has to be a consequence. The expectations need to be set up front, that way it's not a surprise and nobody feels they weren't treated fairly. It's just black and white.

The key to successfully implementing this system is clear communication from the get-go. Everyone on the team should understand the expectations and potential consequences before they even start.

The conversation is simple: If you, as the sales rep, don't hit your numbers in a timely manner within the timeframe we've agreed on, there will be consequences. This creates a fair and transparent environment where success is rewarded and underperformance is addressed promptly. This balance of carrots and sticks helps maintain a high-performing sales team that consistently drives results for your business

As we wrap up this chapter on mastering sales, let's recap the essential elements we've covered:

1. The importance of simplicity in your sales process.
2. Implementing a consistent, repeatable sales methodology like Be REAL or The Home Doctor TECHNIQUE.
3. Leveraging videos to build trust and credibility.
4. Using your CRM to automate and enhance your sales funnel.
5. Balancing rewards and consequences to drive performance.

Remember, the goal isn't just to close a deal—it's to create a system that consistently turns leads into satisfied customers. By focusing on these key areas, you're not just improving your sales numbers; you're laying the foundation for sustainable, long-term growth.

Sales mastery is just one piece of the puzzle in building an eight-figure business. While a strong sales process is crucial, it's equally important to ensure that the promises made during the sales process are fulfilled—and exceeded—after the sale.

This brings us to our next stop on this roadmap to eight figures. In Chapter 10, we'll explore how to truly set your business apart from the competition. We'll dive deep into creating a culture that puts the customer at the center of everything you do, and separates you from the competition. You'll have the tools to not just meet your customers' needs but to create raving fans who become your best marketers. You'll understand how to build a reputation for quality and service that makes your competition irrelevant.

So, as you move forward, keep in mind that mastering sales is just the beginning. You're going to want to see what happens when you combine a killer sales process with an unbeatable customer experience.

Remember:

1. Simplicity is key in sales. Create a clear, repeatable process that your entire team can follow consistently.
2. Implement a structured sales methodology like Be REAL or The Home Doctor TECHNIQUE, adapting it to fit your specific business needs.
3. Leverage video presentations to build trust and credibility, addressing potential objections before your sales rep even starts their pitch.
4. Use your CRM to automate follow-ups and tailor communications to address specific customer concerns.
5. Create compelling, interactive sales presentations using tools like Canva or Ingage to guide your reps through the sales process.
6. Analyze sales performance data to continuously refine your process and provide targeted coaching to your team.
7. Balance rewards for success with clear consequences for underperformance, setting transparent expectations from the start.

CHAPTER 10

Winners Focus on Winning

I t's not just about making sales or delivering a product—it's about creating a customer experience that makes them feel good. In this chapter, we're going to explore two key areas that separate the average businesses from the industry leaders: building a customer-centric culture and providing exceptional quality and customer experience.

By mastering these areas, you'll not only set yourself apart from the competition, but you'll also build a loyal customer base that will fuel your growth for years to come. I'll give you a golden nugget early in this chapter; one of your focuses as the owner should always be *putting distance between you and your competitor.* Make sure that you are so far ahead that it's an easy decision for clients to use you, review you, and refer you.

Core Concerns

Over the years, we've had the privilege of working with thousands of clients. We've also had the opportunity to help thousands of other business owners, particularly contractors, who've also served hundreds of thousands of homeowners. Through all of this, we've gained some powerful insights into what really matters to customers.

We've identified four core concerns in our "Why Cornerstone" video that consistently come up when property owners are dealing with a business or contractor. First and foremost is communication. It's amazing how many problems can be solved or avoided altogether with clear, consistent communication. The second concern is timeliness—being on time and finishing on time. Nothing frustrates a customer more than delays and missed deadlines. The third concern revolves around trust, specifically when it comes to money. Homeowners want to feel confident that they're not being taken for a ride. Finally, the most obvious concern is actually fixing the problem they hired you for in the first place.

Now, you might be thinking, *Well, duh! Of course, these are important.* But knowing what's important and actually delivering on it are two very different things. That's why in all of my companies we put a massive emphasis on customer experience and satisfaction. We're not just talking about delivering a high-quality product (although that's certainly part of it). We're talking about the whole package—being on time, finishing on time, and communicating well throughout the entire process; they're non-negotiables.

Taking Action

So, how do you actually foster this kind of customer-centric culture? One of the biggest factors for us was creating a position within our company specifically focused on customer care. You might hear about customer care positions in massive corporations, but it's not something you typically see in a smaller company, which is something we wanted to change.

We created a dedicated customer care position—someone whose sole job is to be there for our homeowners. If they have any need at all, any concern, any question—no matter how big or small—this person is there to help anytime they need assistance. It might sound simple, but the impact has been huge.

Here's why we did it: We were selling a ton of jobs, sometimes hundreds in a month, and while that's great for business, we realized we had a problem. People would book a job with us and then not hear from us for a couple of weeks.

Now, it wasn't that we'd forgotten about them or were doing anything wrong—it was just taking time to get materials or schedule the job around weather or waiting on an insurance company to do their part. We even tell them up front, "Hey, it's going to be six weeks before we can start the job." And they understood that—at first.

Then the sales reps would get busy and forget to check in, so after not hearing from us for a few weeks, our clients started to think we'd forgotten about them. We were losing jobs because of it. I'm not talking about a few jobs here and there—I'm talking about over seven figures' worth of revenue all because we weren't communicating frequently enough with our homeowners. That's when we knew we had to make a change.

After creating the Customer Care Specialist role, we now reach out and touch base weekly with our clients. We're making sure that the customer knows we're there, that we haven't forgotten about them, and that if they have any issues at all, we're happy to help.

You may be wondering, *How do I hire for a customer care role?* As mentioned previously, we've found great success in utilizing virtual assistants (VAs) for many roles, including our customer care needs. We seek out VAs who are fluent in English with little to no accent and have excellent communication skills. This ensures that our customers receive clear, professional support, regardless of where our VA is located.

One of the best practices we've discovered is to clearly define the VA's role and responsibilities. For us, this includes:

1. Monitoring Customer Communications: Our VAs keep an eye on incoming customer inquiries via email, chat, and sometimes even social media. They're often the first point of contact for our customers.

2. Updating Lead Tracking Sheets: VAs can be instrumental in keeping your CRM or lead tracking system up to date. They can input new leads, update statuses, and ensure all customer interactions are logged.

3. Lead Source Calculations and Revenue Attribution: This is a crucial task that many business owners overlook because of time constraints. Our VAs calculate which lead sources are most effective and attribute revenue to different marketing channels. This data is invaluable for making informed marketing decisions.

4. Proactive Customer Outreach: We task our VAs with reaching out to customers at key points in their journey with us. This might be a check-in call during the project, or a follow-up after completion to ensure satisfaction.

5. Review Requests: After a job is completed, our VAs contact customers to ask for reviews. This systematic approach has significantly boosted our online reputation.

6. Basic Customer Support: For simple queries or issues, our VAs are equipped to handle them directly. For more complex problems, they know how to bring the issue to the appropriate team member.

Tips on Using VAs

When implementing a VA system, here are a few best practices to keep in mind:

1. Thorough Training: Ensure your VAs understand your business, products, and processes inside and out. Provide them with scripts and guidelines for common situations.
2. Clear Communication Channels: Set up efficient ways for VAs to communicate with your in-house team for situations that require escalation.
3. Regular Quality Checks: Periodically review your VA's interactions with customers to ensure they're maintaining the level of service you expect.
4. Empower Your VAs: Give them the authority to make certain decisions to resolve customer issues quickly. This could include offering small discounts or expedited service when appropriate.
5. FAQs: Provide them with Frequently Asked Questions so they are prepared to answer any questions that come their way.
6. Use Technology to Your Advantage: Implement tools that allow your VAs to seamlessly integrate with your existing systems. This might include CRM access, call forwarding systems, or shared document platforms.

The beauty of using VAs for these tasks is the flexibility and cost-effectiveness it offers. You're able to provide round-the-clock customer care without the expense of a full-time, in-house team. Plus, you can easily scale up or down based on your needs at a fraction of the cost of a US-based team member.

Access Our Go-To Virtual Assistant Service Here: TheRevolt.com/ roadmap

We didn't stop at the customer care position. Instead of just having sales reps helping out with production or quality control when they could, we also built out our Production and Quality Control Teams. These folks are dedicated to going out and helping with any issues that might come up during or after the job.

In the past, we had someone lead production but not a full team that was available in the field. This was another big shift for us. Now, our sales reps don't have to worry about any of the production details or quality control issues. They can focus 100 percent on what they do best—helping homeowners get the new product they need.

These changes might seem small on paper, but they've made a world of difference. We're not just delivering a product anymore; we're delivering an experience that addresses those four core concerns we talked about earlier: communication, timeliness, trust, and problem-solving.

In making our customers happier, we're separating ourselves from the competition. In today's market, you can't just rely on having a good product. Most everyone's got a good product. What sets you apart is how you deliver that product, how you treat your customers, and how you handle problems when they inevitably arise.

By focusing on these areas, by truly putting the customer at the center of everything we do, we've been able to create a reputation that speaks for itself. We're not just another contractor —we're the contractor that cares; the one that communicates; the one that shows up on time and finishes on time; and the one that you can trust with your money and your home.

We understand our reputation is what keeps customers coming back. It's what gets them recommending us to their friends and family. It's what allows us to charge a premium for our services. When people work with us, they know they're not just paying for a product—they're paying for peace of mind.

The More We Grow, The More We Give

Another crucial aspect of building a customer-centric culture and separating ourselves from the competition is our commitment to giving back to the community and being a positive force in the world around us. At Cornerstone, we've always believed in the power of generosity. One of our favorite traditions is our 12 Days of Christmas event. Every year, we make a big production out of giving away something special for each of the twelve days leading up to Christmas. Our team members dress up as Santa Claus, elves, the Grinch, and other Christmas characters to spread joy and excitement while creating memorable experiences that show our community that we care.

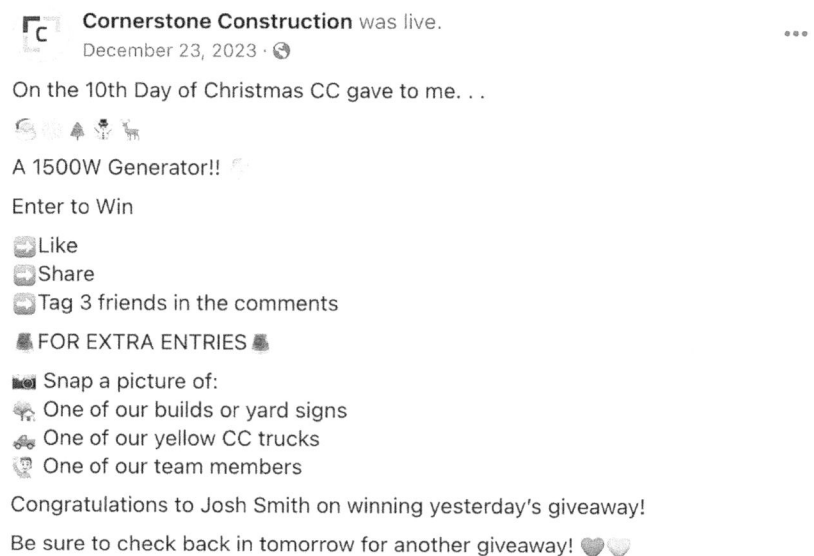

Cornerstone Construction was live.
December 23, 2023 · 🌐

On the 10th Day of Christmas CC gave to me. . .

🦢 🌲 🦌

A 1500W Generator!!

Enter to Win

👍Like
🔄Share
💬Tag 3 friends in the comments

🎁FOR EXTRA ENTRIES🎁

📸 Snap a picture of:
🚧 One of our builds or yard signs
🚚 One of our yellow CC trucks
👷 One of our team members

Congratulations to Josh Smith on winning yesterday's giveaway!

Be sure to check back in tomorrow for another giveaway! 🖤🤍

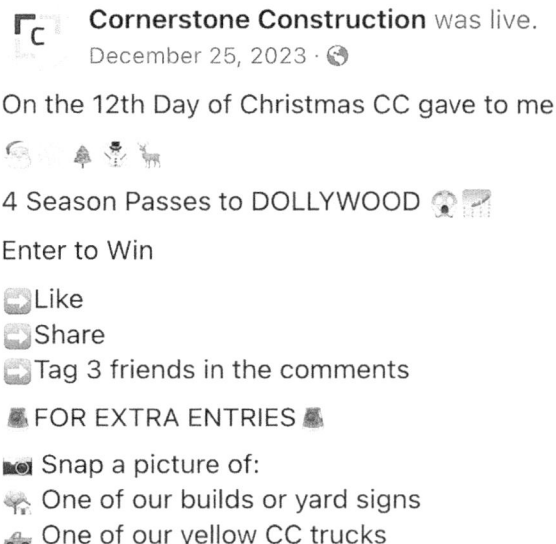

Cornerstone Construction was live.
December 25, 2023 · 🌐

On the 12th Day of Christmas CC gave to me. . .

🎅 🎄 ⛄ 🦌

4 Season Passes to DOLLYWOOD 🎤 🎢

Enter to Win

➡️Like
➡️Share
➡️Tag 3 friends in the comments

🪓FOR EXTRA ENTRIES🪓

📸 Snap a picture of:
🪧 One of our builds or yard signs
🚚 One of our yellow CC trucks
👷 One of our team members

Congratulations to Bailey Banks on winning yesterday's giveaway!

Be sure to check back in tomorrow for another giveaway! 🤍🤍

Our giving doesn't stop at the holidays. We've organized skydiving getaways and cabin retreats, providing unforgettable adventures for our community members. We've also made significant contributions to the Revolt Foundation, which helps underprivileged kids and aligns perfectly with one of our core mottos at Cornerstone, "The more we grow, the more we give." These might seem unrelated to our service, but they're integral to who we are as a company. We're not just here to fix homes—we're here to lift up our community in every way we can.

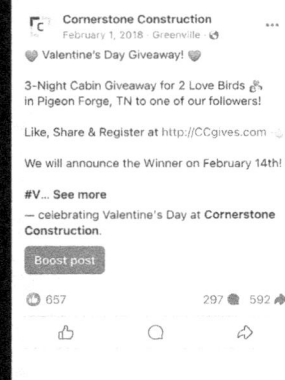

Cornerstone Construction
February 1, 2018 · Greenville ·

♥ Valentine's Day Giveaway! ♥

3-Night Cabin Giveaway for 2 Love Birds 🐦 in Pigeon Forge, TN to one of our followers!

Like, Share & Register at http://CCgives.com

We will announce the Winner on February 14th!

#V... See more
— celebrating Valentine's Day at **Cornerstone Construction**.

Boost post

👍 657   297 💬   592 ➦

Giving back is woven into the very fabric of who we are as a company. We give back because that's who we are at our core. It's not about getting recognition or boosting our image, although those can be nice side effects. It's about making a real, tangible difference in the lives of the people around us.

This commitment to giving back does more than just help the community—it also sets us apart from our competition. In a world where many businesses are focused solely on their bottom line, our dedication to community service shows that we're different and that we care about more than just making money. It shows we care about making a difference.

And you know what? Customers notice this. They appreciate doing business with a company that gives back. It builds trust, loyalty, and a sense of connection that goes beyond the typical business-customer relationship. In essence, our commitment to giving back isn't just good for the community—it's good for business too.

So, as you're building your business and looking for ways to stand out from the competition, don't underestimate the power of giving back. Find causes that align with your values just like we discussed when talking about your common mission. Create traditions of generosity. Make giving a core part of your company culture. Because at the end of the day, the most successful businesses aren't just the ones that make the most money—they're the ones that make the biggest positive impact on the world around them. Refer back to Chapters 1 and 2 for inspiration on giving back in your community.

"Winners Focus on Winning"

Michael Phelps is undoubtedly one of the greatest Olympians of all time. With a total of twenty-eight medals, including twenty-three gold medals across four Olympic Games, Phelps has set a record that seems almost unbreakable. His dedication to his sport and his laser focus on winning have made him a legend in the world of swimming and sports in general.

Back in the 2016 Rio Olympics, Phelps was racing Chad le Clos from South Africa in the 200-meter butterfly. Le Clos had beaten Phelps in this same event in the 2012 London Olympics, which added an extra layer of drama to their 2016 rematch. Leading up to the race, there was significant media attention on the rivalry between Phelps and le Clos, with le Clos making some confident statements about his ability to beat Phelps again.

As they approached the final stretch during the race, le Clos looked over at Phelps, seemingly trying to gauge where his rival was. Phelps, on the other hand, remained laser focused on the wall ahead, never taking his eyes off his goal. And do you know what happened?

Phelps went on to win the race, reclaiming the gold medal that le Clos had taken home four years earlier.

Credit: David Ramos/Getty Images

This moment spawned Eric Thomas' now-famous quote, "Winners focus on winning. Losers focus on winners." It perfectly encapsulates the mindset that separates champions from the rest. Phelps's unwavering focus on his own performance, rather than on his competitors, is a testament to his winning mentality.

The lesson here for us business owners is profound. It's easy to get caught up in what our competitors are doing—their successes, their strategies, their growth. But the true path to success lies in focusing on your own goals, your own performance, your own finish line.

This doesn't mean ignoring the competition entirely. It's okay for them to succeed in their own right. If they serve 1,000 homeowners or get 1,000 five-star reviews, that's great for them. But for me, that means I'm focused on doing even better and setting my goals even higher. I'm serving 2,000 homeowners, getting 2,000 five-star reviews. I want to win. I want to be the greatest. Like I said in Chapter 1, my fifth Life

Law is about chasing greatness. I want to be as good as I possibly can be. To do that, I'm focused on getting myself and my team there, not focusing on how and when the competition is doing it.

Follow-up Processes

Creating effective follow-up processes for your homeowners allows you to deliver an exceptional customer experience. In order to streamline this process and ensure consistent, timely communication with your clients, let's dive deeper into how you can leverage technology – particularly with your CRM like we talked about in the previous chapter.

Automations in your CRM are time-savers when it comes to customer follow-up. If your CRM already has built-in automation capabilities, that's fantastic. You're sitting on a gold mine of potential for improving your customer communication. If not, don't worry—there are ways to add this functionality.

One powerful tool for creating these automations is Zapier. It's a platform that allows different software applications to "talk" to each other, creating workflows that can save you countless hours of manual work. By connecting your CRM with other tools through Zapier, you can create a seamless, automated communication system.

Here's How This Might Work in Practice:

Let's say a homeowner's job status changes in your CRM. Maybe you've just scheduled their installation date. Instead of having a team member manually reach out to the customer with this update, you can set up an automation that triggers a text message and/or email to the homeowner as soon as that status change occurs in the CRM.

For example, you could create an automation that says, "When a job status in the CRM changes to 'Scheduled for Installation' *and* an installation date is added, send a text message to the customer with the following message, 'Great news! Your installation has been scheduled for [Installation Date]. If you have any questions, please don't hesitate to reach out.'"

This automation accomplishes several things:

1. It ensures the customer is informed immediately about updates to their project.
2. It reduces the chance of human error or forgetfulness in communication.
3. It frees up your team's time to focus on other important tasks.
4. It provides a consistent communication experience for all customers.

Don't stop at installation dates. Here are similar automations you can create for various stages of the customer journey:

- When a quote is prepared and ready for review.
- When materials have been ordered for their job.
- When the crew is on the way to start the job.
- When the job is completed and ready for final inspection.
- When the warranty information has been processed and is ready to send.
- When it's time to request reviews and referrals.

Each of these touchpoints is an opportunity to keep your customer informed and engaged, building trust and demonstrating your commitment to transparency and communication. Look at all of the stages of your pipeline and tailor automations to fit your specific business's processes.

You can also use these automations to gather feedback, which we'll dive deeper into shortly because this is imperative on its own. For instance, you could set up an automation to send a satisfaction survey a week after job completion. This not only gives you valuable feedback but also shows the customer that you care about their experience even after the job is done.

The beauty of this system is that it takes the manual work out of follow-up communication. You're no longer dependent on a human remembering to make that call or send that email. The system does it automatically, ensuring that no customer falls through the cracks.

Moreover, this automated system allows for speed and consistency in your communication. Every customer gets the same high level of communication, regardless of which team member is managing their project. This consistency is key to building a strong, trustworthy brand.

Remember, while automation is powerful, it shouldn't completely replace human interaction. Use these automated touchpoints as a foundation, and then layer personal, human communication on top through your sales reps, project managers, and/or customer care. For instance, your automated text about a scheduled installation could be followed up by a personal call from the project manager to address any specific questions or concerns.

By combining the efficiency of automation with the warmth of personal interaction, you're creating a customer experience that's both high-tech and high-touch. You're ensuring that your customers are always in the loop, always feeling cared for, and always experiencing the best possible service.

Customer Feedback

Continual customer feedback is absolutely critical for any business that wants to grow and improve. You shouldn't just bask in the glow of positive reviews; you should seek out all types of feedback, especially from those customers who aren't thrilled with your service. As much as it might sting to hear criticism, these dissatisfied customers are often your greatest source of valuable insights.

As soon as a job is completed, our VA on the customer care side reaches out to the homeowner to get a review. When a customer is unhappy, that's your cue to lean in, not back away. Ask them directly what they're not satisfied with, and probe deeper to understand how you can improve. These conversations, while potentially uncomfortable, are gold mines of information that can help you refine your processes, improve your products, and enhance your overall customer experience.

A complaint can actually be a gift. It's an opportunity to turn a negative experience into a positive one, and more importantly, it's a chance to turn an unhappy customer into a raving fan, while also allowing you to prevent similar issues from occurring with future customers. By actively seeking feedback from unhappy customers, you're demonstrating that you value their opinion and are committed to making things right. This approach can often turn a detractor into an advocate for your business.

Tony Robbins has emphasized the importance of customer feedback to refine and improve his offerings from early on, saying, "Feedback is the breakfast of champions. It's the information that helps us grow and get better." So, don't just ask for feedback—act on it. Use the insights you gain to make real, tangible improvements in your business. This could mean tweaking your processes, providing additional training to your team, or even overhauling entire aspects of your service. When customers see that their feedback leads to actual changes, it builds trust and loyalty.

Attendees of Robbins's seminars and programs are encouraged to share their thoughts on the content, delivery, and overall experience. Based on his attendee feedback, he's made enhancements to his events such as: content customization, improved engagement, and enhanced support materials. By seeking and implementing feedback, he's been able to build a loyal following and sustain his reputation in the personal development industry.

How Can a Strong Company Culture be Developed to Enhance Customer Experience?

Developing a strong company culture that enhances customer experience is indeed crucial for any business aiming for long-term success. You can't just talk about culture; you have to live it every day through your actions and decisions.

There are several key components at the core of a healthy company culture that prioritizes customer experience:

1. Servant Leadership: This philosophy, championed by business leaders like Ken Blanchard, puts the needs of employees and customers first. It's about leaders asking, "How can I help?" rather than simply giving orders. By modeling this behavior at the top, it filters down through the entire organization.
2. Selflessness: This ties in closely with servant leadership. It's about putting the customer's needs above your own immediate gains. Sales reps shouldn't view customers as mere dollar signs or commission checks. Instead, they should genuinely want to help and provide value.

3. Hospitality: This goes beyond just being friendly. It's about creating a welcoming environment for both employees and customers. Tony Hsieh of Zappos was famous for fostering a culture of hospitality that extended from how employees treated each other to how they interacted with customers.

4. Professionalism: This doesn't mean being stuffy or formal. Rather, it's about consistently delivering high-quality work and maintaining high standards in all interactions.

5. Growth Mindset: Popularized by psychologist Carol Dweck, a growth mindset allows for continuous improvement. It encourages employees to view challenges as opportunities to learn and grow, rather than insurmountable obstacles.

6. Customer-Centricity: This means putting the customer at the center of everything you do. Jeff Bezos of Amazon is well known for his customer-centric approach, even leaving an empty chair in meetings to represent the customer.

Our approach to reinforcing this customer-centric mindset at Cornerstone is to refer to customers as part of the "Cornerstone Family." In doing so, we've created a mental shift where employees naturally want to treat customers' properties as if they were their own.

To develop and maintain this kind of culture, consider these strategies:

1. Lead by Example: As a leader, embody these values in your day-to-day actions. Your team will follow your lead.

2. Hire for Cultural Fit: When bringing new people on board, look for those who already align with your core values. Skills can be taught, but cultural alignment is harder to instill.

3. Regular Training: Conduct ongoing training sessions that reinforce your cultural values and show how they apply in real-world customer interactions.

4. Recognize and Reward: Highlight employees who exemplify your cultural values, especially in their interactions with customers. This reinforces the behavior you want to see.

5. Create Rituals: Establish company rituals that reinforce your culture. This can be enforced in your weekly team meetings where you share customer success stories, or an annual awards ceremony that celebrates exceptional customer service.

6. Empower Employees: Give your team the authority to make decisions that benefit the customer. This shows trust in your employees and allows for quicker resolution of customer issues.

As the legendary management consultant Peter Drucker once said, "Culture eats strategy for breakfast." You can have the best business strategy in the world, but without a strong, customer-centric culture to execute it, you'll struggle to achieve lasting success. By fostering a culture of servant leadership, selflessness, and customer-centricity, you're setting your business up to not just satisfy customers but to truly delight them. Just remember, culture isn't something you can force or create overnight. It's cultivated over time through consistent actions and reinforcement.

Closeout

Let's recap the key points we've covered in our journey to build a customer-centric culture and separate ourselves from the competition. First, we started by identifying the four core concerns of customers: communication, timeliness, trust, and problem-solving. Second, we explored how to address these concerns through various strategies, including creating a dedicated customer care position, improving our quality control processes, and leveraging technology for better communication. Third, we delved into the importance of automating follow-up processes using CRM systems and integration tools like Zapier, ensuring consistent and timely communication with customers. Fourth, we emphasized the critical role of customer feedback in driving business improvement, using examples of successful business leaders who have made this a cornerstone of their operations. Next, we learned that even negative feedback is a gift, providing valuable insights for growth and improvement. Then, we explored the use of virtual assistants in customer care, discussing best practices for integrating them into your business to provide round-the-clock support and manage crucial tasks like lead tracking and review solicitation. Finally, we dove deep into the importance of company culture in enhancing customer experience.

Throughout this chapter, we've seen that winning in business is about consistently delivering exceptional value and experiences to your customers, and focusing on your own goals while continually striving to improve, rather than getting distracted by what others are doing.

As we are getting closer to the end of our roadmap, we'll get into finding leverage for operational efficiencies and how technology can make the back end of your business run like an eight-figure business.

Remember:

1. Put distance between you and your competitors. Make it an easy decision for clients to choose, review, and refer you.
2. Create a dedicated customer care position. It's not just for big corporations—it can revolutionize your business.
3. The more we grow, the more we give. Make giving back a core part of your company culture.
4. Automate your follow-up processes. Use your CRM and tools like Zapier to ensure consistent, timely communication.
5. Feedback is the breakfast of champions. Actively seek it out, especially from unhappy customers.
6. Culture eats strategy for breakfast. Foster a culture of servant leadership, selflessness, and customer-centricity.
7. Hire VAs for customer care. They can handle everything from monitoring communications to requesting reviews.

CHAPTER 11

Thrive, Not Survive

If you've made it this far, you're not just looking to keep your head above water—you're ready to dominate the ocean, and in this chapter, I'm going to show you exactly how to do that. We're diving deep into the world of cutting-edge technology and operational strategies that will streamline your business, boost your productivity, and skyrocket your profits. This chapter isn't just about survival—it's about thriving in a business landscape that's evolving at breakneck speed. It's about using technology, not as a crutch, but as a launching pad to propel your business to heights you've only dreamed of.

Leveraging Technology: My Experience With RepCard

Let me share a personal story about how I've leveraged technology to revolutionize my business operations. In 2021, I became a partner in a business called RepCard, and it's changed the way I interact with leads, not just for me, but for over 127,000 professionals in various industries.

RepCard started as a simple digital business card, but it's evolved into something far more powerful. It's now a comprehensive tool for anyone in sales, especially those in the door-to-door space. Imagine having a mini funnel-builder right in your pocket—that's what RepCard has become.

Here's how it works:

1. Customizable Profiles: You can set up your own handle (mine is app.repcard.com/hunter) where people can view your profile, but that's just the tip of the iceberg.

2. Tailored Offerings: The real power comes in creating specific cards for different offerings. Let's say you're in pest control. You can create a card with call-to-actions, videos, and follow-up campaigns all tailored to pest control. If you're in solar, you can do the same thing with solar-specific content. You can build these while talking to the customer, understanding their specific needs in under thirty seconds.

3. Real-Time Alerts: Anytime someone interacts with your card—views it, clicks a link, watches a video—you get an alert. This allows you to reach out at the perfect moment, when they're actively engaged with your offering.

4. Automated Follow-ups: RepCard handles the follow-up process for you. No more forgetting to send that crucial second or third message. The system does it automatically, keeping your prospects engaged without extra effort on your part.

5. Competitions: One feature I'm particularly excited about is the ability to create competitions within RepCard. You can have your sales reps compete against each other or set up team competitions. It's a great way to gamify the sales process and boost motivation.

6. Control of the Conversation: Here's where RepCard really shines compared to other digital card solutions. With tap cards using NFC chips, when you share your info, the

homeowner gets your details, but you don't get theirs. With RepCard, you're sending them your card. The conversation goes something like this, "Hey, I don't have any physical cards on me, but I do have my digital business card. Can I send it to you?" They usually say yes because it doesn't raise any red flags, allowing you to have their contact info and control the follow-up.

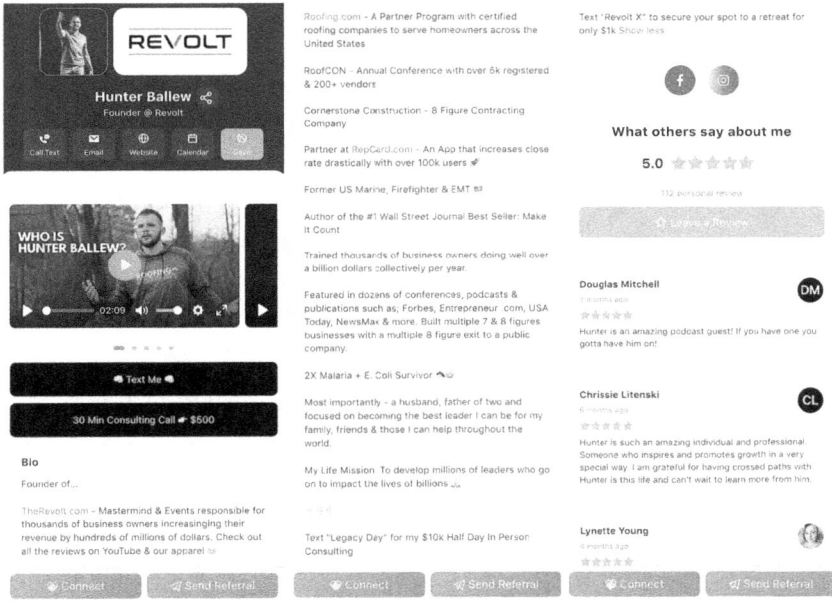

This approach puts the power back in the hands of the sales rep. You're not just handing out your information and hoping for a call back. You're initiating a connection, providing value through your customized card, and setting the stage for follow-up interactions.

I've seen RepCard transform the way sales teams operate. It's not just about having a digital business card—it's about having a complete sales and follow-up system in your pocket. Whether you're a solo entrepreneur or managing a large sales team, tools like RepCard can significantly streamline your operations and boost your efficiency.

Leveraging the right technology, like RepCard, can give you a significant edge in today's competitive business landscape, allowing you to work smarter. If you're interested in seeing how this tool can work for your business, you can check out the free version at RepCard.com. Trust me, you're going to be blown away when you see everything it can do.

Leveraging AI

One of the most revolutionary tools available to businesses today is artificial intelligence (AI). If you're not already familiar with AI, it's time to get on board. A great starting point is ChatGPT or Claude, which you can find at chatgpt.com or claude.ai. These powerful AI tools can be your secret weapon for a wide range of business tasks.

Imagine having an assistant that can help you write social media posts, create job descriptions, outline responsibilities, set expectations, and even create KPIs for specific roles. That's just scratching the surface of what AI can do for you. Need to hire? AI can craft a compelling job listing or job description tailored to your needs. Looking to expand your team? AI can write social media posts to attract potential candidates.

There are two key takeaways you need to understand to make the most of this technology:

1. The Power of the Prompt: The quality of AI's output is directly related to the quality of your input. In other words, the more detailed and specific you are with your prompts, the better the AI's response will be. Don't just ask for a "job description." Instead, provide details about the role, the skills required, your company culture, and any other relevant information. The more context you provide, the more tailored and useful the AI's output will be.

2. The 90/10 Rule: This is a big one, so make sure you understand. AI is not about perfection—it's about efficiency. Think of AI as a team member whose job is to get you 90 percent of the way there. Your job is to take that 90 percent and refine it, adding your personal touch to make it perfect. Don't expect AI to produce flawless, ready-to-use content every time. Instead, view it as a powerful first draft that you can then tweak and polish while saving you hours on end.

AI does the heavy lifting, freeing up your time and mental energy to focus on the final touches that require human insight and expertise. It's not about replacing human creativity or decision-making; it's about enhancing it.

Once you've either downloaded the app or gone online and created an account, you want to start customizing. The more you use it, the more it will get to know you. For example, in ChatGPT, you give it information about yourself, and it will give you prompts, such as: Where are you based? What do you do for work? What are your hobbies and interests?

Uploading any of your own writing from things like posts or transcripts helps it to mimic your tone and sound more like "you."

Let's look at creating a social media post with ChatGPT for hiring a sales rep. In the prompt, we have: "Can you create a social media post to hire a sales rep for my roofing company? The offer is a truck provided with a wrap and ladder along with training material and training pay for the first two months. They will be 1099 with no salary and a 10 percent commission. Our average rep earns $104,000 per year in commission." This covers all the basics of what we offer our sales reps right out of the gate. You should get even more specific with required experience, responsibilities, and so on, but here's a starting point.

ChatGPT's response: Sure! Here's a social media post to hire a sales rep for your roofing company:

Join Our Team as a Sales Rep!

Are you a driven and motivated individual looking to earn a lucrative income in the roofing industry? We have an amazing opportunity for you!

Position: Sales Representative
Company: [Your Roofing Company Name]
Location: [Your Location]

What We Offer:

- A company truck, complete with a professional wrap and ladder.
- Comprehensive training materials.
- Training pay for the first two months.
- 10 percent commission on sales. (Our average rep earns $104,000/year in commission!)
- 1099 contractor position with the flexibility to manage your own schedule.

Why Join Us?

At [Your Roofing Company Name], we believe in setting our team up for success. With the tools and training provided, you'll have everything you need to excel and grow in this role. Our supportive environment and high earning potential make this an opportunity you won't want to miss!

Responsibilities:

- Generate leads and develop new business.
- Provide outstanding customer service and build lasting client relationships.

- Present and sell roofing solutions to potential customers.
- Meet and exceed sales targets.

Requirements:

- Excellent communication and interpersonal skills.
- Self-motivated and goal-oriented mindset.
- Ability to work independently and as part of a team.
- Previous sales experience is a plus but not required.

If you're ready to take the next step in your career and join a company that values your hard work and dedication, apply now!

Email your resume to: [Your Email Address]

Call us at: [Your Phone Number]

Visit our website: [Your Website URL]

Join us at [Your Roofing Company Name] and start your journey to success today!

#SalesRep #Hiring #RoofingSales #JoinOurTeam #SalesOpportunity #RoofingJobs #SalesJobs

—

What if I want it to sound more like "me"? I'd ask it to edit the post and do exactly that.

New prompt: Can you edit that to sound a little more personal and a little more "me"?

—

ChatGPT's response: Absolutely! Here's a more personal and engaging version:

Join Our Family as a Sales Rep!

Hey there! Are you a go-getter looking to earn big in the roofing industry? We've got an incredible opportunity just for you!

- **Position:** Sales Representative
- **Company:** [Your Roofing Company Name]
- **Location:** [Your Location]

What We Offer:

- A sweet company truck with a custom wrap and ladder.
- All the training materials you need to succeed.
- Paid training for the first two months.
- A solid 10 percent commission on sales. (Our reps average $104,000/year in commission!)
- 1099 contractor position, giving you the freedom to be your own boss.

Why You'll Love Working With Us: At [Your Roofing Company Name], we're more than just a company—we're a family. We give you the tools and support you need to shine and grow. With a high earning potential and a supportive environment, this is a gig you don't want to miss!

What You'll Do:

- Find and develop new business leads.
- Deliver top-notch customer service and build strong client relationships.
- Present and sell our awesome roofing solutions.
- Crush your sales targets and reap the rewards.

What We're Looking For:

- Stellar communication and people skills.
- A self-starter with a goal-driven mindset.
- Someone who can work independently but also loves being part of a team.
- Sales experience is great but not a must—we train you!

Ready to join a team that values your hard work and dedication? Let's chat!

Send your resume over to: [Your Email Address]

Give us a call at: [Your Phone Number]

Check us out at: [Your Website URL]

Come be part of [Your Roofing Company Name] and start your journey to success today!

#SalesRep #Hiring #RoofingSales #JoinOurFamily #SalesOpportunity #RoofingJobs #SalesJobs

---

See how this sounds just a little more personable? Again, the more you use it, the more it "gets to know you."

Now let's say you're creating a marketing campaign. You can use AI to generate initial ideas, draft copy, and even suggest targeting strategies. That might get you 90 percent of the way there. Then, you step in to refine the messaging, ensure it aligns perfectly with your brand voice, and add those unique touches that resonate with your specific audience.

By adopting this mindset, you'll find that AI becomes an invaluable tool in your business arsenal. It's not about relying on AI to do everything, and it's not to replace your expertise or judgment— it's about leveraging its capabilities to boost your productivity and creativity. It's like another brain to help you when you need it.

Call Centers

A tool that can help you scale, but is not discussed often, is a call center. This approach has allowed me to scale my lead generation efforts while keeping costs remarkably low.

In a couple of our businesses, I've implemented a call center setup with five full-time callers and a dedicated manager, all based overseas. These professionals are laser focused on setting leads and appointments, creating a steady stream of opportunities for our sales team to convert. The efficiency is impressive, but what's truly remarkable is the cost-effectiveness. We're paying pennies on the dollar compared to what we'd spend for similar services stateside.

You might be wondering about the complexities of setting up such an operation. The good news is you don't need to be an expert in international business to make this happen. There are professionals who specialize in establishing and managing these overseas operations, handling everything from recruitment to training to ongoing management. The beauty of this model is that you can start with one or two VAs making calls or go all in with an entire team and dedicated manager.

Within this call center framework, we've also integrated VAs to handle a variety of supportive tasks. While we've discussed VAs in previous chapters, it's worth noting how they complement our call center operations.

The synergy between our overseas call center and our VA team has created a powerhouse of productivity. Our call center focuses on the core task of lead generation, while our VAs handle the supporting tasks—updating our CRM, handling follow-up communications, and assisting with customer care—that keep our sales funnel flowing smoothly.

One of the key benefits of this setup is its scalability. As our business grows, we can easily expand our call center team or increase our VA support, allowing us to meet increasing demand without the typical growing pains of expansion—for a fraction of the cost.

In Cardone's book *The 10X Rule,* he discusses how he used offshore call centers to dramatically scale his business operations. Cardone set up a call center in India to handle inbound sales calls for his online training programs. Initially, he was skeptical about whether non-native English speakers could effectively sell his American-focused content, but he was pleasantly surprised by the results.

By providing rigorous training and implementing strict quality control measures, Cardone's offshore team began to outperform many of his U.S. sales representatives. The offshore team's dedication, work ethic, and ability to work flexible hours allowed Cardone's business to provide 24/7 sales support, significantly increasing conversion rates and overall revenue.

I understand that thinking about venturing into 'overseas operations' might seem daunting if you're new to it. That's why I want to extend an offer: If you have any questions about setting up a call center, integrating VAs into your operations, or even finding the right recruiters for these roles, feel free to reach out to me directly on Facebook Messenger. I'd be more than happy to answer your questions or connect you with the exact people I use for these services.

Remember, in today's global economy, building an efficient, scalable business often means thinking beyond your local talent pool. By leveraging and integrating virtual support, you're creating a robust, flexible system that can adapt to your business needs and help drive your growth to new heights. It's about working smarter, and these tools are a perfect example of how global connectivity can transform the way we do business.

Revisiting Key Areas for Automation and Customer Experience Enhancement

As we continue our journey toward operational efficiency, it's worth revisiting some crucial areas where automation and technology can make a significant impact. While we touched on these in the previous chapters, their importance warrants another look.

Areas Ripe for Automation

When considering where to implement automation in your business, several key areas stand out:

1. Lead Nurture: Automating your lead nurturing process ensures that no potential customer falls through the cracks. It allows for consistent, timely follow-ups without requiring constant manual intervention.
2. Follow-up: Whether it's after a sale, a service call, or an initial inquiry, automated follow-ups keep your business top of mind for customers and prospects alike.
3. Customer Care Touches: Regular, automated check-ins can make customers feel valued and attended to, even when your team isn't directly interacting with them.
4. Cross-sales: Automated systems can identify opportunities for additional sales based on customer data and behavior, triggering targeted offers at the right time.
5. Review Request: Automating the process of requesting reviews can significantly increase the number of positive reviews your business receives, boosting your online reputation.

Enhancing Customer Experience Through Technology

When it comes to using technology to improve customer experience, one area stands out above the rest: customer care. This is where technology can truly shine in making your customers feel heard, valued, and never forgotten.

Imagine a customer's journey through your sales pipeline. At each stage, they receive an automated message updating them on their status. These messages could be as simple as:

"We've received your inquiry and are reviewing it. Expect to hear from us within twenty-four hours."

"Great news! We've scheduled your consultation for [Date]. Click here to add it to your calendar."

"Your project is now in the planning phase. Here's what to expect next . . ."

"We're excited to let you know that your project is scheduled to begin on [Date]. Here's what you need to know to prepare."

These automated touches serve multiple purposes:

1. They keep the customer informed, reducing anxiety and the need for them to reach out for updates.
2. They demonstrate that you value the customer's time and understand their need for information.
3. They create a sense of progress, even during phases where not much may be visibly happening from the customer's perspective.
4. They reduce the workload on your team, freeing them up to handle more complex customer interactions.

Remember, when working with homeowners—or any customer, for that matter—one of their biggest fears is being forgotten or ignored. By implementing these automated touches, you're constantly reassuring them that they're a priority, that their project is moving forward, and that you're there if they need anything.

This approach to customer care is about making customers feel good and creating efficiency. By proactively providing information through automated channels, you're reducing the number of inbound inquiries your team has to handle, allowing them to focus on more complex issues and high-value interactions.

While we've discussed these points before, they bear repeating because of their profound impact on both operational efficiency and customer satisfaction. By focusing your automation efforts on these areas, you're creating a customer experience that sets you apart from the competition.

Balancing Innovation and Stability: The Art of Measured Implementation

While we've discussed numerous exciting technologies and strategies to boost your business efficiency, it's crucial to remember one vital principle: Don't try to implement everything at once.

Change, even positive change, can be disruptive. Your sales reps and team members are on the front lines, day in and day out, working hard to meet their targets and serve your customers. While we want them to adapt and improve continually, we also need to be mindful of their capacity to absorb new information and processes.

Imagine you just got five new ideas from the past three chapters that could revolutionize your business. You're excited, and rightfully so, but if you try to implement all five simultaneously, you risk overwhelming your team. Your sales reps might find themselves spending more time learning new systems than actually selling. Your support staff might be struggling to keep up with a constantly shifting workflow. The result? Frustration, decreased productivity, and potentially, a hit to your bottom line.

Remember, your team's primary job is to sell and serve customers. While we want them to adapt and get better, we also don't want to bog them down so much that they can't effectively do their core job. It's a delicate balance.

So, how do you strike this balance? Here are a few strategies:

1. Prioritize: Evaluate which new implementations will have the biggest impact on your business. Start with those. Add each to your project management tool with a deadline based on importance.
2. Phased Approach: Instead of rolling out multiple changes at once, implement them in phases. This gives your team time to adapt to each change before moving on to the next. Remember, this book is written as a roadmap to follow. Use it to its designed intent.
3. Pilot Programs: Before company-wide implementation, test new technologies or processes with a small group. This allows you to work out kinks and gather feedback before scaling up.
4. Clear Communication: Explain to your team why you're implementing these changes. When people understand the "why," they're more likely to embrace the "how."
5. Training and Support: Provide comprehensive training for new tools and processes. Ensure ongoing support is available as your team adapts.

6. Feedback Loop: Create channels for your team to provide feedback on new implementations. This not only helps you refine your processes but also makes your team feel heard and valued.

7. Celebrate Small Wins: Acknowledge and celebrate when your team successfully adapts to new changes. This positive reinforcement can help build momentum for future improvements.

Remember, the goal is continuous improvement. It's okay to be excited about new possibilities, but it's equally important to be strategic about how and when you implement them.

By taking a measured approach to implementation, you're more likely to see successful adoption of new technologies and processes. Your team will appreciate the consideration, and you'll be able to more accurately assess the impact of each change in your business. In the end, it's about how effectively you can integrate improvements to drive your business forward. So take a breath, prioritize, and implement with purpose.

As we wrap up our exploration of ways to not just survive but thrive, it's clear that these tools and strategies have the power to transform your business. From AI and automation to overseas call centers and streamlined customer care, these innovations create a more responsive, agile, and customer-centric business.

You can have the most streamlined operations, the most advanced AI, the best overseas team—but without a clear vision, you're just spinning your wheels if you don't know where you're heading. That's why in the next chapter, we're going to zoom out and bring it all together by bringing clarity to your vision and discussing how to execute it. Because, at the end of the day, all these tools and strategies we've discussed are just that—tools. They're a means to an end, not the end itself.

So, I want you to start thinking big. What's your ultimate vision for your business, and how do you get there using all that we've covered so far? What legacy do you want to leave? These are the questions we'll be grappling with as we bring everything we've learned together into a cohesive, actionable plan for success. Let's finish strong and set you up to not just survive, to not just succeed, but to truly thrive in your business and leave a lasting impact on your customers, your team, and your family.

Remember:

1. Winners leverage technology to put distance between themselves and competitors.
2. The power of AI lies in the quality of your prompts and the 90/10 rule; let AI do 90 percent of the work, then refine it.
3. Overseas call centers can dramatically scale your operations at a fraction of the cost.
4. Automate key areas like lead nurture, follow-ups, customer care touches, cross-sales, and review requests.
5. Enhance customer experience through regular, automated updates throughout their journey.
6. Implement new technologies and processes gradually to avoid overwhelming your team.
7. Balance innovation with stability—your team's primary job is still to sell and serve customers.

CHAPTER 12

The Path Forward

We've gone over how your vision is the north star of your business. It should guide every decision, every strategy, and every action. It's what gets you out of bed in the morning when things are tough. It's what inspires your team to go the extra mile. It molds together your core values, common mission, mission statement, and it's what sets you apart from your competition.

A vision without execution is just a dream. That's why in this chapter we're not only going to help you clarify your long-term vision, but we're also going to give you the tools to execute it effectively.

Why is establishing your long-term vision so important? Because without a clear vision, all the strategies and tactics we've discussed are like arrows without a target. They might be sharp, they might fly fast, but without a definite goal, they'll never hit their mark. So, by the end of this chapter, you will have written out your long-term vision and created a clear path that you, your team, and others can rally behind—giving you a clear path forward. This isn't just an exercise—it's the culmination of everything we've discussed; the blueprint for your future success.

Taking Action

All right, it's time to roll up our sleeves and get to work. We're going to create a concrete plan for your business's future, right here, right now.

We're about to begin an exercise that will shape the future of your business and establish your exit plan. I want to make sure you're giving this section your full, undivided attention because it's an idea that many people automatically brush off, but this is concept should be woven into your long-term vision.

The Exit Plan

A lot of people have no idea what it looks like to exit a business, and many times people say, "Oh, I would never sell my business. I love it too much," or, "I want to leave it to my kids," or, "I want to keep it for cash flow." The reality is that you're going to exit your business at some point in some way – you sold it, you gave it away, you died.

I know some of you are thinking, *Hunter I've got plenty of years left in me. In fact, I'm just starting out. Do we really need to talk about an exit strategy now?*

This might seem premature, especially if you're just starting out, but trust me, having an exit strategy shapes everything, even if you don't think you need one. It's better to build your business in a way that it's prepared to sell when the unexpected happens than to need to sell and not be ready.

When I start talking about selling for $10, $20, $50 million, it usually catches the attention of people who "aren't interested in selling." They start thinking, "If I could get that kind of cash, spend more time with my family, and spend my time doing something I enjoy more than what I do now, maybe I actually would be interested in selling." Not only that, but you start thinking about the possibilities available when you have that kind of money, the impact you can make on the world around you when you have that kind of financial freedom.

So, ask yourself:

- Do you want to hold your business for cash flow?
- Do you want to give your business to your children?
- Do you want to sell your business one day?
- What do you want your business to be worth when you sell it?
- When do you want to sell?

Once you have that end goal, you can work backward by asking yourself:

- What valuation metrics do you need to hit? (Revenue, EBITDA, Multiple)
- What systems need to be in place?
- How can you make your business attractive to potential buyers?

The Value of Exploration

I think the above questions are worth at least looking at because you don't have to commit to selling your business to consider them, to dive deep into your true reasons for those answers. Furthermore, understanding what an exit could look like opens up possibilities you might not have considered before because it puts you in a position of strength, and gives you that option, whether you choose to follow through with a sale or not.

Remember, having an exit plan means you're prepared for whatever the future might hold and have options that will allow you to control your business's destiny, no matter what life throws your way.

How many people do you know who've not only built a business, but they *are* the business? Without them, the business doesn't run. When it comes time to retire, or the unexpected happens and they can no longer run the business like they always had, they don't have an exit plan, they don't have anything to sell, and the business just crumbles, so they're left with nothing.

This is what we want to avoid. I understand the thought of selling something you put your life's work into can be scary. I'm just encouraging you to be prepared, and work with the end in mind, even if it never happens.

You've probably heard the saying, "Everything has a price." I live my life that way. Almost everything has a price. When I got a call about a company being interested in buying Cornerstone, I had zero desire to sell it. But I decided to follow through with the meeting to at least learn the process, sharpen my negotiation skills, and understand how due diligence works. By the end of it, I was looking at an offer of $48 million that I couldn't turn down.

As we work through this exit planning exercise, I'm just asking you to keep an open mind. You might be surprised at the opportunities that present themselves when you start seriously considering what your business exit could look like. Take your time with this exercise, don't rush it, and really think through each step. Visualize your success. Feel it. Then plot out how to get there. Remember, these plans aren't set in stone. They're living plans that you'll revisit and revise as circumstances change and you grow.

Let's do a basic walk-through of company valuation.

The *Clarity Calculator*—remember, you can use this resource to help reverse engineer exactly what metrics you must hit to achieve your revenue goals and enterprise value goals. Your enterprise value is what you could sell your company for.

Access The *Clarity Calculator* Here: TheRevolt.com/roadmap

It's important that you know your company's specific metrics and the industry averages when it comes to multiples based on earnings before interest, taxes, depreciation, and amortization (EBITDA) ranges.

Most companies are valued on a multiple of their EBITDA or seller's discretionary earnings (SDE). In this case, we'll use EBITDA. You'll be able to add interest, taxes, depreciation, and amortization back on top of your net profit when doing your valuation.

But wait, there's more. You get what is called "add backs." Simply, think of these as one-time expenses that the company won't have to make in the future under new ownership. A great example of this is the annual membership cost for Revolt community members. The new owner doesn't have to continue with our community to get the same result. So, the owner is able to add that fee back to the profit before the valuation is done.

I'll give an example I've seen in the contracting space.

Let's say you have a company that does $5 million a year in revenue and your EBITDA is 10 percent, which works out to $500K.

It's likely you'd get a 3x on your EBITDA.

Meaning, three times $500K, which works out to $1.5M, plus assets (we'll leave assets out of these examples, as they will vary, but know they will be added).

Here's where the compounding effect really comes into play and makes an exit sexy. If you double the revenue, double the EBITDA, and double the multiple, you do not just double the enterprise value. It's much greater.

Let's double each and see what the enterprise value works out to.

$10M a year in revenue at 20 percent EBITDA, which is $2M, times 6x.

Now your enterprise value is $12M. You went from $1.5M to $12M. An 8x in enterprise value by simply doubling each of the three. This is the power of understanding where you need to be and casting the long-term vision based on that.

Let's do one more example.

$20M a year in revenue at 20 percent EBITDA, which is $4M, times 8x.

Now, we have grown the enterprise value to $32M by doubling the revenue, keeping the EBITDA margin the same, and increasing the multiple by 2x.

Use the *Clarity Calculator* to understand exactly where you need to be in revenue, EBITDA and multiple to hit your exit goal.

Now you know what's possible and can hone in your vision to include being prepared for an exit.

The Power of Annual Review

I want to really hone in and make sure you understand the importance of regularly reviewing and updating your vision and mission. I'm not saying you have to do that weekly or monthly or even quarterly, but every year in January, I personally like to dial in and look at the mission that we have within our company. I'm also looking at my personal mission statement and making sure that I'm still in alignment with that. For me, it's a long-term life mission statement that I have. It's not necessarily changing, but I want to make sure that I'm doing the things that I need to do to accomplish it.

January serves as the perfect time to reassess and refine your vision for the year ahead. It's a natural point of reset, allowing you to reflect on the past year's achievements and challenges, and set a clear direction for the coming year.

One additional step I take in January is creating a "Word of the Year" for myself and the team—a word that sets the tone for the entire year, and one we mention frequently. This year, our word was "attitude." Have a positive attitude in all situations whether we're dealing with problems or clients, and also have a get-crap-done attitude. No excuses. Only solutions. We reference it throughout the year and let it set the tone for our team.

It's important to remember that while your overarching vision might be set annually, your strategies to achieve that vision should be reviewed and adjusted more frequently. That's where the quarterly strategy sessions come in.

Quarterly Strategy Sessions

These quarterly check-ins are vital for several reasons:

1. They allow you to assess progress toward your annual goals.
2. They provide an opportunity to adjust tactics based on what's working and what's not.
3. They keep your team aligned and focused on the vision throughout the year.

Prepare for the next growth phase, including setting new goals and strategies for continuous improvement. Again, strategies are going to change in between. You're going to realize things don't work, or things are working better than you thought they would. While your vision provides a stable north star, your strategies need to be agile enough to adapt to changing market conditions, new opportunities, or unexpected challenges. Flexibility is crucial.

To effectively review and update your vision and mission, consider the following steps:

1. Market Analysis: Regularly assess your market. What trends are emerging? How are customer needs evolving? Your vision should reflect where the market is going, not just where it's been.

2. Team Input: Your team is on the front lines, interacting with customers and dealing with day-to-day operations. Their insights are invaluable. Create channels for ongoing feedback, and make sure to incorporate their perspectives in your vision updates.

3. Customer Feedback: Directly engage with your customers. What do they value most about your business? What needs aren't being met? Their feedback can help you refine your vision to better serve your market.

4. Core Values Check: As you consider changes to your vision or mission, always refer back to your core values. Any updates should align with the fundamental principles that guide your business.

5. Why You Started: Revisit your original motivation for starting the business. Has that changed? If so, how does that impact your vision moving forward?

6. External Perspective: Consider bringing in outside consultants or advisors. Sometimes, an external perspective can highlight blind spots or opportunities you might have missed.

7. Competitive Analysis: Look at what your competitors are doing. How is your vision differentiated? Are there areas where you need to pivot to stay competitive?

Your vision should be aspirational yet achievable, pushing your business to grow while staying true to its core purpose. By combining annual vision setting in January with quarterly strategy sessions and ongoing market awareness, you create a rhythm of continuous improvement and adaptation. This approach keeps your business agile and responsive while maintaining a clear long-term direction. It's this balance of stability and flexibility that allows businesses to thrive in today's rapidly changing market environment.

Expanding Your Vision

As time goes on, as I gain more life experience and new perspectives, I always want to make sure that I'm updating my vision for what's possible. I know there's more out there, and I want that vision to include more and more people that I can serve. And that's what I want for you in your own business.

This is about growth—not just in terms of numbers but in terms of impact and possibility. Don't be afraid to dream bigger and reach further. Your vision and mission are living things. They should grow and evolve as you do. By regularly reviewing and updating them, you ensure that your business remains aligned with your values and goals, ready to adapt to changes while staying true to its core purpose.

Let's look at the constantly evolving vision of a massive company like Amazon. When you look at Amazon, it started as just a bookstore in 1994 because Bezos felt books were easy to source and ship. In 1995, Amazon.com launched, and by 1997, Amazon went public. The initial public offering raised $54 million, giving the company a market value of $438 million. Then in 1999, Amazon began selling music, videos, toys, and electronics. In 2005, they launched Amazon Prime, which now has over 200 million members worldwide.

Today, Amazon is the biggest marketplace in the world, which has allowed Jeff Bezos to become one of the richest men in the world. Throughout this evolution, Bezos maintained his core vision of being "Earth's most customer-centric company." This vision allowed Amazon to expand far beyond its original scope as a bookstore, adapting to new technologies and market opportunities in 2007 with the release of Echo and Alexa. This vision is what keeps Amazon alive and well today.

Embracing Failure as a Learning Opportunity

Some people say, "Sometimes you win; sometimes you lose." I don't like that saying. I prefer Maxwell's, "Sometimes you win; sometimes you learn," or better yet, Jimmy Buffett's, "It's good to learn from your mistakes. It's better to learn from other people's mistakes." The key point: This mindset of viewing failures as learning opportunities is crucial for any entrepreneur. It's not about avoiding failure—it's about embracing it as a stepping stone to success. So remember, as long as you're learning, you're never losing.

Navigating Tough Times

When the market changes and things get tough, it's easy to get upset or feel like you're trying your hardest, and it's just not "working." But the reality is most of us are probably feeling that way.

I've been talking with different people lately, another great example of why you should join mastermind groups or have coaches who can inform you of what others are feeling, and they're like, "Man, retail sales are just down this year. Must be because it's an election year." Then I talk to some of the old dogs that have been in business for forty years, and they say, "Yep, every election year, it's like this. People just get tight on their wallet. They're afraid of what's going to happen to the economy." The point is, if you follow the data and are still struggling, it's likely the whole market, and that's okay.

The Power of Connection

It's important to understand and align yourself with other people who are where you want to be, so you can have outlets to ask those questions. Their experience and insights can be invaluable in helping you navigate challenges, adapt your vision, and stay true to your mission, even in the face of adversity.

You have to be surrounded by the right people for you, your business, your team, your family, your life, and your vision to continue evolving. Because if you stay in a small pond, you might be the big fish there, but when you go over to the lake, you find that you're the small fish. It's what naturally happens if you just stay in your hometown, in your comfort zone, in those small circles. Whereas, when you get around a group like what we have with our Revolt community, you start to think bigger, and everything changes. It's really amazing to see.

So, if you're in a group with a bunch of entrepreneurs that do $500,000 and you do $1 million, you may feel really good about yourself, but you are doing yourself a disservice in the long run. Instead, join a group where everyone's doing $10 million-plus. Not only will you feel like, "Man, I'm not doing good at all," you will feel the pressure to do better, and you will realize what's possible. You will believe that it's possible because you see other people doing it.

John C. Maxwell has written extensively about the importance of surrounding yourself with the right people. In his book *The 21 Irrefutable Laws of Leadership*, he discusses the "Law of the Inner Circle," which states that a leader's potential is determined by those closest to him or her. Maxwell truly believes this because he's lived it. In his early career as a pastor, he intentionally sought out mentors who were leading larger, more successful churches. He would travel to visit these pastors, sometimes just to spend a day observing and learning from them.

Cardone shares this common thread in his approach too: Actively seek out environments and relationships that challenge you to grow. Understand that by surrounding yourself with people who share this drive for excellence and innovation, you set yourself up to continuously evolve your vision and push the boundaries of what's possible in your own business. This mindset of constant growth and adaptation is what has driven the success of many of the leaders we've talked about.

Here's why this approach is so powerful:

1. Diverse Perspectives: By putting yourself out there through groups, personal development, etc., you're exposing yourself to a wide range of perspectives. This diversity of thought can help you spot trends or potential market shifts that you might miss if you're only looking at things from your own viewpoint.

2. Collective Wisdom: These groups often include people who have been in the industry longer than you have. Their collective experience can serve as an early warning system for market changes. They've likely weathered various market cycles and can recognize the signs of impending shifts.

3. Extended Network: The people you meet in these groups aren't just valuable for their own knowledge. They often

have connections to other industry experts, analysts, and thought leaders. By being part of these groups, you're essentially tapping into a much larger network of knowledge and insight.

4. Real-Time Information: Industry conferences and online groups often discuss current trends and emerging issues in real time. This can give you a significant advantage in spotting and adapting to market changes quickly.

5. Reduced Isolation: If you're only focused on your local market or immediate circle, you might miss broader industry trends. These groups help you break out of that isolation and see the bigger picture, so you don't feel lonely as an entrepreneur.

6. Opportunity for Collaboration: Sometimes, adapting to market changes requires new partnerships or collaborations. By being part of these larger industry groups, you're well positioned to form strategic alliances when needed.

Being part of these communities can help alleviate fears about market changes. When you're connected with others who have successfully navigated similar challenges, it becomes easier to see market shifts as opportunities rather than threats. You're no longer facing these changes alone, but as part of a knowledgeable, experienced community.

Remember, in business, knowledge is power. By leveraging the collective wisdom of your industry peers and mentors, you're empowering yourself to not just survive market changes but to thrive through them. This proactive, community-oriented approach to market intelligence is a key factor in long-term business success and resilience. While surrounding yourself with others within your industry is powerful, I believe it to be equally important to surround yourself with those outside your industry. Why? You are able to take full advantage of what other industries are doing and be the first to innovate in your industry.

The Power of Vision Boards

"Should I make a vision board?" I *absolutely* think you should. They're a powerful tool for manifesting your goals and keeping your team aligned. They provide a tangible, visual representation of your aspirations, making them feel more real and achievable because you are looking at them and updating them daily with real-life results. We have high-quality printed vision boards that we hang on the walls for each of our companies after we set our goals and begin working toward them.

For instance, with our conference, RoofCON, if we want to sell 200 vendors, we have a board made with 200 seats that represent 200 vendors for that year. Then throughout the year, we're filling in each spot with the name of each vendor that signs up. These can be designed on canva.com for free and printed at a local print shop.

The point of having the board is having a visual and engaging reminder, which creates a sense of momentum as we see the spots filling up. It turns our goal into a game, making the process more enjoyable and motivating for the whole team.

Using vision boards in your business is a powerful recruiting and motivation tool. It shows potential team members that you have a clear direction and ambitious goals. It helps them see themselves as part of something bigger.

When a candidate would come in to interview for the job, I'd pull up the vision board and say, "Hey, here's the vision. This is how we're going to grow. Here are the markets we want to be in. Here are how many reps we need. This is how much money we're going to give back to the nonprofit. This is how many people we're going to serve . . ." I just share the vision and let the boards help them realize I'm not just spouting words, that I actually have a plan in place and am working toward what I say.

This approach makes it so that you're not just offering a job; you're inviting them to be part of a mission. You're showing them that your company has a purpose beyond just making money. When people see that, belief is instilled in them because they know that you're serious about it. It's not just a job where they're going to come and say, "Oh, just another job, working day to day. I guess I'll do this, and then at some point, I'll get tired and go get another job." No, they want to be a part of the mission and seeing it through.

People are increasingly looking for work that has meaning beyond just a paycheck. By highlighting how your company gives back, you're tapping into that desire for meaningful, purpose-driven work. This is the power of a well-communicated vision. It turns employees into partners who are invested in the success of the company because they can see how their work contributes to a larger goal.

As we wrap up this chapter on clarity, vision, and execution, remember that your journey as an entrepreneur is an ongoing process of growth, adaptation, and refinement. By regularly reviewing and updating your vision, creating tangible representations like vision boards, and surrounding yourself with experienced mentors and peers, you're setting yourself up for long-term success. Your vision isn't just a destination—it's a guiding light that illuminates your path forward, inspiring both you and your team to reach new heights.

In our final stop, we'll explore the personal journeys of entrepreneurs who have implemented the strategies and principles we've discussed throughout this book. These real-world examples will bring to life the concepts we've covered, showing you how others have navigated the challenges and triumphs of building a thriving business. So, get ready to be inspired by their stories and to see how you can apply these lessons to your own entrepreneurial journey.

Remember:

1. Establish a clear long-term vision for your business, including an exit plan.
2. Regularly review and update your vision, mission, and strategies through annual reviews and quarterly sessions.
3. Use tools like the *Clarity Calculator* to understand and plan for your company's valuation.
4. Embrace failure as a learning opportunity and navigate tough times by understanding market trends.
5. Surround yourself with mentors and peers who challenge you to think bigger and grow.
6. Create vision boards to visualize your goals and use them as powerful recruiting and motivation tools.
7. Your vision should evolve as you gain experience and uncover new possibilities for your business.

CHAPTER 13

The Realization of What is Possible

Welcome to the final chapter, our final stop on this roadmap to eight figures. This chapter is designed to show you what's truly achievable when you apply the frameworks and tools we've discussed throughout this book. To do this, I've asked some entrepreneurs from the Revolt community to share their journeys from start to finish. Some of them have built companies generating over $10 million in annual revenue, while others have led businesses that sold for over a billion dollars.

As you dive into these stories, remember that each of these entrepreneurs started somewhere. They weren't born special or destined for success from day one. What sets them apart is their willingness to learn, adapt, persevere, and apply the principles we've discussed in this book.

Get ready to be inspired, challenged, and motivated. You'll read about their impressive victories, but you'll also learn about the challenges they faced, their moments of doubt, and the obstacles they had to overcome. Because for every win celebrated, there are usually many losses that were encountered behind the scenes. I believe it's crucial to acknowledge that real business isn't the highlight reel you often see on social media. This is the reality of building a successful business, and it's important that you understand and prepare for it. So, let's turn the page and see what's truly possible when you commit to building something extraordinary.

From Bankruptcy to Billions: Jonathan Cronstedt's Roller-Coaster Ride to a $2 Billion Empire

www.jcron.com

Hunter is a good friend of mine, and when he asked me to talk about the realization of what's possible, I had a lot of thoughts. For one, it's so much easier to connect the dots looking backward. Know that while on this journey, I had nowhere near the clarity or certainty that this summary has.

Since you've gotten to this point in the book, I want to say congratulations. The vast majority of people don't read. They don't have a vision for their life that's compelling enough to pull them into doing what is necessary to progress. The very fact that you've read this far in the book, I want to congratulate you and share one of my favorite quotes. Jim Rohn said, "Poor people have big TVs; rich people have big libraries." I'm glad that you've invested in what is either your first, or maybe one of many, books that is going to powerfully impact your life.

I'd also like to share an idea that makes success unique. It's one of the few things in life you commit to buy, but you won't know the price until after you've paid it. So wherever you are on the journey, I hope my story can help.

Let me share with you about what my price of success has been. I can remember when I moved to Southern California from the midwest suburbs outside of Chicago and I was confronted by the fact that I was dropped into one of the wealthiest enclaves of the United States. A bit of a culture shock for a Midwest kid, I always knew I wanted to achieve more, but now I was surrounded by it. I now saw what was possible, but I wasn't yet sure how to get there.

Thankfully, I found my first mentor by dropping a note inside of a 1997 black Lamborghini Diablo Roadster. He told me I needed to learn to sell, and that was my first step on this journey that took me into automotive sales. I then parlayed my sales abilities into a mortgage career in which I thought I had realized success. I thought I had gotten to the mountaintop. I was making more money than I'd ever imagined, and so I 100 percent financed a bunch of real estate because everyone knows real estate doesn't go down and smart people invest in real estate (or so I thought). Then in 2007, the mortgage company went bankrupt. All of the houses were underwater and worth less than the purchase price, so the houses, the cars, everything went back to the bank. My job was gone, and I had the joy of filing for bankruptcy.

After realizing that the mortgage days weren't coming back, I bought Dan Kennedy's "whole enchilada," which was four boxes of products on direct response marketing. This led to my digital marketing career, and I was extremely blessed to have run into amazing mentors along the journey. I had the pleasure of working with and being mentored by Joe Polish, Matt Bacak, Chet Holmes, Tony Robbins, Mike Koenigs, Ryan Deiss, Roland Frasier, and others on this journey that ultimately led to my favorite season of my entire career: getting to go to work with my best friend Kenny Rueter, who was the cofounder and CEO of kajabi.com, an online learning and marketing automation platform.

I was able to join the company in 2016 as partner and president, and we were doing about $6 million in annual recurring revenue at the time. Over the next five years, we would grow from $6 million in revenue and twenty-five team members, to over $100 million in revenue and 400 team members. The platform has now powered over $7 billion earned by the creators that are on it and a $2 billion valuation with Tiger Global, TPG, Owl Rock, Meritech, and Tidemark on the team. It was truly an incredible journey. Kenny and I moved from our operating roles to board positions in July of 2021.

Over the last four years, I've had the opportunity to learn what it means to lead from a board-level position. I was able to retire three months before my fortieth birthday. It's allowed me to be home with my wife and my now four-year-old daughter, and for me, the measure of success has been being able to provide options in my life and have the schedule with my family that I wish my parents had been able to have. I wish my dad had had the opportunity to choose—to choose to have a more open and flexible schedule, to not need to travel five days a week, to not always be on the road.

So for me, I started this journey believing that success would be defined by material things. For a large period of my journey, it was those items that drove me. However, now I've come to find that those things don't really offer fulfillment or excitement or long-term joy. I've come to appreciate time a whole lot more—an empty calendar, lunches with my wife, swim classes with my daughter. Time is the ultimate luxury.

I hope for all of you reading, that you have the same opportunity. I hope that all of you experience enough success that you get to have your own existential crisis (I certainly did). Regardless of my warning about the disorienting effect of success, I know you're going to want to experience it for yourself. I know I did. Your success story is in process, and I look forward to hearing about the forthcoming victories.

From Farm Fields to Rooftops:
Brian Ward's Journey to Eight Figures

You know, I never thought I'd end up running any sort of a multimillion-dollar company when I was growing up in Allentown, Florida. It's this tiny farming community with maybe 500 people, one blinking light, and a single K–12 school. I graduated in a class of thirty-two kids, if that gives you an idea.

My entrepreneurial spirit? I picked that up from my family. They weren't just farmers—they were diversified businesspeople, even if we didn't see it that way or call it that.

My dad, uncle, grandpa, and his brothers, they didn't just grow one crop. All together, they had one to two thousand acres where we grew peanuts, cotton, soybeans, pecans, grass hay, and a huge family garden. We even raised several hundred head of cattle—you name it. In addition to farming, my dad worked a career with the county's road and bridge department and even had a rental property with four units. Without really knowing it, I was watching my family, my dad in particular, create multiple income streams.

Our family garden was something else. It wasn't just for us—it was for my grandpa, all his brothers, their kids, my aunts, uncles, and all their kids. We're talking about a twenty- to thirty-acre garden. Every weekend during harvest season, we'd all get together to pick corn, peas, butter beans—you name it. It was like an event, all of us working together to put up the harvest, creaming corn, shelling peas. We'd do this over the course of several weekends, until every family had what they needed for the year.

My first real taste of business came when I was about fifteen. After the family had taken what they needed, there was still plenty left in the garden. My dad encouraged me to collect what was left and sell it in town. I'd go to Miss Bass's restaurant or the Winn-Dixie, selling fresh veggies I'd picked myself. By sixteen, I was making an extra $200 to $300 a week. Not bad for a kid, right?

In high school, I did pretty well without really trying. Small school, you know? I even did some dual enrollment and had a year's worth of college credits when I graduated. I had it all planned out—a six-year plan to become an anesthesiologist. But God had different plans for me.

Three weeks before I turned nineteen, Hurricane Ivan hit. I'd just started working for a local roofing company in what was supposed to be a temporary job between semesters. Suddenly, I was thrown into the deep end. Ivan was a high-end Category 3, and it devastated the area. The gentleman I was working for offered to double my salary and pay production bonuses if I stayed instead of going back to school. Before I knew it, I was making $2,000 to $3,000 a week as a lead man on a metal roofing crew. School got put on the back burner really quick.

By twenty, I'd bought my first house and decided to start my own business: Quality Roofing. Talk about bad timing. I'd picked the worst possible moment to start a roofing company. We'd just had back-to-back hurricanes, Ivan and Dennis. About 95 percent of the roofs in the area had just been replaced. Those first ten years were tough, let me tell you. I did windows, doors, siding, decks, fences, gutters, patios, kitchens, baths—just about anything to make ends meet.

I hit rock bottom a few years in. I think I got a little too comfortable, maybe having a bit too much fun in my early twenties. Woke up one morning to find my truck repossessed, a stack of bills I couldn't pay on the counter. I was behind on my mortgage and nearly lost my home. I had to swallow my pride and borrow $20,000 from my dad just to keep afloat. That was a wake-up call.

Things turned around slowly. I started putting in serious hours, wearing every hat in the business. My then fiancée, Melissa, gave me an ultimatum one night as I worked away on estimates into the late hours—hire some help or find a new fiancée. That push got me to make my first hire, and I moved the business out of the spare bedroom and into the garage to accommodate a second desk—a small, but meaningful step at the time.

Those first ten years were slow and tough. But looking back, it was probably the best thing that could have happened. I matured at the same pace as the company. We grew organically, adding a crew here, a few more people there. In 2015, we finally moved out of the garage into a small office in a strip mall.

One of the first real game-changers for me was hiring my now CRO, David, in 2017. He was the first legitimate salesperson I ever had, and he doubled our revenue in a year, from $4 million to $8 million. Then Hurricane Michael hit in 2018. David and I basically slept on the office floor for months, picking up $5 million to $6 million worth of roofs in just that short period of time, helping us close that year out in our very first eight-figure year, at $13 million. Working that storm, a couple of hours away from our home market, delivered one of the most important lessons I've learned in business—the value of relationships. Without two key relationships and referral sources, we would have been lucky to pull off $2 million to $3 million from that storm.

2020 was shaping up to be another record year. Demand was booming as we were approaching the peak of the replacement cycle for all of the roofs that had been replaced after the very same hurricanes that pulled me into the industry. Then COVID hit, and believe it or not, it was great for the home service industry. We were pacing for $20 million— and then, on the sixteen-year anniversary of Hurricane Ivan, Hurricane

Sally arrived. After that storm, things were crazy busy, as you'd expect. In the midst of all this, I was invited to one of Hunter's free retreats. I almost canceled—we were swamped. But Hunter convinced me to come, and I'm so glad I did. That retreat was a game-changer. It gave me access to so many tools and strategies that were crucial for the next phase of our growth.

2021 was a banner year for us, hitting $30 million. But 2022 brought new challenges. Our revenue actually dipped a bit, down to just north of $20 million. Now, this might sound bad, but there was more to the story. Our market was naturally constricting after the storm, but our market share was actually growing. We were capturing more of the available reroof jobs than ever before. I made sure to dig into the data to understand what was really going on.

At the same time, we were expanding. We opened new locations in the Destin area to our east and in Orlando as well. Of course, these were just getting started and weren't contributing much to our revenue yet. But we were laying the groundwork for future growth.

2023 was a year of building momentum. Our new markets started gaining traction, and we were still growing our market share in Pensacola. We finished the year at $24 million in revenue. One of the most pivotal things that happened that year was the hiring of my now COO, Ryan. He's a fantastic integrator and has been an incredible asset, really driving so many positive cultural and operational changes and giving me the opportunity to work closely with one of my very best friends.

In 2023, we set an audacious goal and cast the vision for growing the organization from three locations and $25 million to thirty locations and $150 million by the end of 2026. It's a huge goal and we know that, but we've also spent countless hours reverse engineering every detail of the plan and understanding exactly what needs to happen and how we will get there.

Today, we are pacing for $35 million in 2024, have grown to six locations and expect to have nine locations by the end of the year. In 2025, we have a plan to open three new locations per quarter with a revenue target of $60 million. We will continue that pace in 2026 to achieve the $150 million target, as the strategically chosen locations continue to individually grow.

It hasn't been easy—every new level brings its challenges, and it's fair to expect hurdles that we can't yet see. As I like to say, every level has a different devil. You grow until you hit the maximum capacity of your team, then you reinvest, which impacts the bottom line in the short term, but it expands your capacity and ability to continue growing.

Looking back, I wouldn't change a thing. From watching my family juggle multiple income streams on the farm to selling veggies to running this company, every step has taught me something valuable.

I'm so grateful for my blessings, my friends, my family, and all of the great people like Hunter who've supported me and provided guidance just when I needed it most. I'm especially thankful for the amazing team at Quality Roofing, the opportunity and platform God has given us to do so much good.

We do our best every day to live by our mission statement: "To consistently build, grow, and nurture an organization that gives priority to the continual growth and development of all who serve it. We will challenge the status quo and bring positive and impactful change to the communities we serve."

From East London Bricklayer to Concierge for Billionaires: Steve Sims's Journey

www.stevedsims.com

I never had one of those dramatic, overnight success stories. My journey was more like a series of dominoes—little hinges that moved big doors. It all started in East London, where I was just another working-class lad. I was a bricklayer, getting up at four in the morning, coming home at eight at night, beaten up, cut up, and dead tired. I knew what hard work was, but I had no clue about smart work.

Back then, I was rolling around on a crappy motorcycle that only occasionally started. My nights usually ended at the local pub, where my mates and I could only afford two or three beers before heading home. That constant state of being broke, of wanting more but not knowing how to get it—that was my fuel. It was pure aggravation.

One night, everything changed. We were leaving the pub, trying to kick our bikes into life, when this nice car pulled up. Now, it wasn't a McLaren or anything, but to me, on my beat-up bike, it might as well have been Richard Branson in a Rolls-Royce. This guy steps out wearing nice slacks and a shirt, reaches into the back seat for his jacket—I swear, it was like slow motion. Then a beautiful girl gets out of the passenger seat. I thought to myself, *That's the life I want.*

So, what did I do? I ran at the guy, full speed. Now, picture this: I'm 245 pounds of ugly biker. You don't want me running at you. I yelled, "Hey, how come you are rich and I'm not?" I really wanted to know. I wanted him to spill everything—how he did it, how he saw relationships, opportunities, all of it.

Instead, he jumped back in his car and took off like a bat out of hell. My mates were on the floor laughing. One of them said, "Look at you. You've just scared the shit out of that guy. Who would talk to you?" That's when I caught a glimpse of myself in the pub window. I realized there was nothing wrong with my question, but everything was wrong with my delivery.

That moment taught me one of the most valuable lessons of my life: If you want a great answer, ask a great question—and ask it the right way. I learned to approach people differently. Instead of charging at them, I'd say, "Excuse me, I'm just wondering, how do you see success? And how come so many people have it and so many don't?"

This change in approach opened doors I never imagined. I started meeting successful people who were willing to share their wisdom. I soaked it all up like a sponge. I learned about smart work, about seeing opportunities where others saw obstacles.

Fast-forward, and I ended up founding the world's most successful concierge firm for millionaires and billionaires. I became known as the "make-it-happen" guy for the rich and famous.

But here's the thing—none of this would have happened if I hadn't been willing to ask questions, to be curious, to seek out knowledge from those who had what I wanted. And more importantly, if I hadn't learned how to ask those questions in a way that made people want to answer.

My journey from that East London pub to rubbing shoulders with some very powerful people on the planet taught me this: Success isn't just about hard work. It's about smart work, curiosity, and the willingness to help others. It's about being aggravated enough with your current situation to do something about it, but smart enough to approach change the right way.

So, if you're reading this and you're where I was—frustrated, wanting more, but not sure how to get it—start by asking questions. Be curious. Be willing to learn. And remember, it's not just what you ask but how you ask it that can change your life. That's how a bricklayer from East London became the go-to guy for billionaires. And if I can do it, trust me, so can you.

Forging a Roofing Empire From Humble Beginnings: Stephen Maassen's Journey

Well, I can say I never thought I'd be running a multimillion-dollar roofing company. For years, I was just working to pay my bills, $10 an hour forever basically. I landed in the steel fabrication industry, and I thought that was going to be my life. My life was great. I was making $80,000 a year, and I was going to be there long term. I continued to get my $1, $2 raises a year every other year, and I was content with that.

I busted my ass seventy, eighty, sometimes ninety hours a week, basing everything off of overtime. Anytime the heater broke or the AC broke or something had to get fixed, my wife and I would have to get together and figure out how we were going to pay and what we were going to do to make it work.

Then, unexpectedly, I lost that job. Well, I was fired from that job, to be quite blunt, and I kind of didn't know what to do with my life. I found a job selling roofs. I went in for an interview, and they hired me. After a very short time period of selling roofs, I started getting customer complaints. I know now it's nothing out of the norm, but they weren't getting taken care of in a quick manner, so I felt bad. These were my homeowners. So I started getting up on the roof and fixing their fascia, or I'd go to Lowe's and start replacing gutter guards.

Once I started pricing stuff out, I started seeing these profits, and thought, *Wow, this company is making a fortune off of me.*

So I put my two weeks in. And then in May of 2021, I got my LLC. Needless to say, I was ambitious and did not realize what I was getting myself into. I thought I'd just be a general construction company. I picked up a landscaping job, just some random ins and outs. Man, I was busting my back. Then, shortly after, a big hailstorm hit locally, and I was stuck finishing this landscaping job. I kicked myself in the butt. I'd missed a golden opportunity. Right then, I decided: no more of anything else. I'm strictly going after insurance restoration jobs.

The goal was simple: make enough money for my family to live comfortably. I figured, I'm used to $80,000, so if I could work part-time and double that, we'd be set. What I didn't realize was that I'd signed a non-compete with my old company. They found out I started my own business and slapped me with a lawsuit. I got served papers telling me what I was doing was illegal and to shut down.

I was lost. By the grace of God, a family member stepped in and vouched for me with the attorney. We eventually settled, agreeing that I'd stay out of that specific county for six months. But man, it was defeating. No one even trained me at that company. Zero training. I was just told to go knock doors, and now they were trying to tell me I couldn't provide for my family? I didn't know whether to shut down or give up. But I pushed through, and thank God I did.

That first year was what I consider a tank. I'm a recovering alcoholic, and I threw it all away and started drinking. I was drinking every day from 7:00 a.m. until night. This was six months into my journey, and my family was relying on me. My wife basically gave me her blessings to chase my dreams and start a business, and I was letting her down.

By the grace of God, a buddy from AA stepped in. He told me, "Get in rehab. I'll take care of all your jobs. I'll install your roofs. I'll be there for the installs." I don't think I'd be where I'm at today without him.

After getting out of rehab, I took AA very seriously, and I approached my business with the same intensity. I dove in, researching and developing my craft. My buddy from AA noticed what I was doing and eventually joined me as my first employee. I thought he'd come in and sell all these roofs for me, but he had his own struggles. I was the one selling a bunch of roofs, getting better every day.

At this point, I was just trying to make an okay living for my family so we didn't have to stress over the heater, AC, or new tires. Then another guy from my previous company wanted to join us. When he came on board, it lit a fire under my first employee. Suddenly, we had three of us slinging roofs, and we hit $1.5 million in our second year.

We started taking it very seriously, focusing on how to use the CRM and supplement claims better. With my production background, Kyle's love for people in sales, and Adam's roofing knowledge, we made a really good team.

But I hit a roadblock when a customer's lawyer brother looked up my name and found my past drug and alcohol charges. It was nothing serious, but there were past charges. And it was enough for that customer to not want to use my company. I was defeated and started hiding my last name on my cards. I was hiding from myself.

Then I went to one of Hunter's retreats. I was hoping for some secret sauce to hit eight figures, but what I got was way more valuable. I heard a guy share his story about overcoming his past, and it was a wake-up call. I realized I needed to own who I am. That night, I burned those cards with my fake name in the fire. From then on, I stopped hiding. I am who I am.

Hunter even let us visit his Arkansas location, which is unheard of in this industry. Seeing his operation made me think, *If he can do it, why can't I?* We hired another sales rep, and the company hasn't looked back since. We went from $300,000 in that first year when I was drunk half the time, to $1.5 million, to $8.5 million, and now we're on track for $16 million.

It hasn't been easy, though. Learning to handle employees has been a challenge. I'm very macho, "tell it like it is," and not everyone responds well to that. One of the hardest things I have had to do as an owner was letting Kyle go. It started as just an employer/employee relationship, but then he became someone I would consider a best friend. Two months after letting him go, a huge hail storm hit, and his first call was to me asking me for just one more opportunity to work this one hail storm. I was very hesitant, but in the end, I let him back on board out of loyalty, and man, he sold $1.3 million in one month. Since that moment, he's been an example of what a salesman, leader, and father should be. Needless to say, Kyle is still a part of the team today. That was one of the worst things and best things to have to do in my company. I've witnessed that, in a way, I have come to realize I have the duty and the power to change people's lives.

Today, my life is completely different. It's a blessing. I always say, "I'm just some dumb-dumb who happened to get some really cool people willing to follow me." I never anticipated it being what it is today. Now, our goal is to be the best and largest roofing company in St. Louis.

Three years in, we're debating how to grow from $16 million to $25 million, then to $50 million. I'm running numbers through my head, wondering if $12 million is a large enough valuation for my company. That's something I could never have imagined before.

The look in my mom's eyes when she tells me she's proud of me, or being able to pay for someone to cut my dad's ten acres of grass every week—you can't plan for this kind of stuff. I used to be the loser son they were constantly bailing out of jail. Now, I'm living a life I never dreamed possible.

If you have a dream, follow it. But know this: I run this company like an obsession. No one is going to work harder than me. You're not going to start your company and sit back after a year or two. You've got to grind it out. I ran on extremely low overhead for the first two years, doing everything myself until there weren't enough hours in the day. Only then did I bring on help—my wife was able to quit her job to work for the company.

That's my advice: Be prepared to work harder than you ever have before. But if you stick with it, man, the rewards are beyond anything you could imagine.

Unleashing Potential: Blake Anderssen's Self-Made Journey to Pet Industry Millions

I'm the founder and CEO of Pet Parents. Today, we have about a dozen employees, a 46,000-square-foot office, warehouse, and retail store that we built a couple years ago. We've been north of eight figures for the last five years.

But where I started was far from where I am today. I grew up incredibly poor—the whole nine yards, food stamps, going hungry at night. Both my parents were never married, and were hardcore drug addicts and then, eventually, alcoholics. From birth to age three, I was with my mom while my dad was in prison. Then I lived with my grandparents from three to ten, with my mom from ten to fifteen, and then my dad from fifteen to eighteen. A college football scholarship brought me out to Iowa from California, and in a sense, here we are.

What I have today has everything to do with my belief, but it's not as if I had any investors, a rich dad, or an uncle to help me. What really started it was the fact that I grew up poor, played football competitively in California, and I couldn't get a normal job. So I turned to entrepreneurship because it was the only way that I could make money without trading my time. I would go to school, go to football practice, and then late at night, I would jump on a computer that my mom had won at work, and I would work till 2:00 a.m., go to sleep, school, repeat this process.

Because of that, I started in the early 2000s when SEO (search engine optimization) was a lot easier than it is today. I had a few writers in India, understood the basics of SEO, and I basically sold my services. Once I got a contract from a website owner or someone needing content, I would hire or pay my freelancers in India to complete the work. That's where I kind of started. That got me into SEO and entrepreneurship.

Since then, I've had an SEO business, a cell phone case drop-shipping retailer way back before it was really easy with all the new software, I sold candy bars and energy drinks from my backpack in high school, I had a nightclub event company in college, a software development company, and a few different e-commerce stores before leading to Pet Parents. All those had different degrees of success—some I came out well ahead, and some just didn't go anywhere, so I went to something new.

The point is, I've done a couple different things. I didn't just get lucky with one thing. I didn't have success out of the gate, and I did not have support in the sense of someone else to give me money, give me resources, or even to teach me. I really only have one meaningful lesson from my father, which was, "If you want to be a loser, hang around losers. And if you want to be a millionaire, hang around millionaires."

Besides that, a lot of my learning is self-taught, observing from my parents what not to do instead of what to do, and just being a lifelong learner, always trying to learn and adapt and grow myself individually.

At the age of fourteen, I decided to be an entrepreneur, and essentially, ever since then, I have been. I'm now thirty-one, going to be thirty-two in a few months. You could start, quite literally, with alcoholic, abusive parents, food stamps, nothing. And then, in my case, be a millionaire by twenty-five and a multimillionaire by twenty-seven, and have many years of eight figures. And for us, hopefully one day, nine figures.

To help others starting out or those already on the journey, I want to share a couple things. First off—and I tend to be a no-nonsense, kind of direct communicator—there is no secret sauce. It's literally that simple. You're not going to find a shortcut. Similarly to eating healthy and working out, we all know we should eat less fast food and work out more often. We know what to do, but taking action and having the discipline to stick with it through the ups and downs is the hard part.

Another thing I found to be helpful is leaning into a natural belief for me, which is that no one is going to save you. It's on you. You need to be competent at every facet of your craft. This is especially important in the early stages, but all the way up to eight figures and beyond. In the early stages, you're going to quite literally be doing everything yourself. And you need to understand these things fairly well in order to do them. That means learn, do research. We're taught in school a lot of times to go to our teachers, or go to our coaches, or go to our mom and dad, or whatever it may be. But at the end of the day, they're not going to do your homework; they're not going to make that play. And for most parents, you know they're not going to—or I would argue they shouldn't—step in and buy that car, that house, or that investment.

So realizing and accepting that it is on you, and you individually have to understand how to get there and act accordingly, is really important. But in order to do that, you have to be competent in the areas that you need to be for your business or for your craft. So continue to learn. Go out and learn. Learn your stuff. Continue to learn your things.

Additionally, if you're on your way to eight figures and beyond, in order to scale, you've likely heard something like, "Don't work in your business, but on your business." This is true, but you do need to be competent in every aspect so you can effectively lead other people, and you can effectively spot good and bad talent.

For example, a sports coach needs to know what a good offensive lineman and a good wide receiver look like, how they behave and perform on the field, in order to effectively coach. The point is to develop your understanding and experience in every aspect of your business. As you scale, you'll bring on position coaches and hire players, but because you're competent in those areas, you'll be able to spot a good position coach or offensive line, or a good offensive or defensive coach.

Too often, I observe others who are always seeking a new book, new learning, you know, some guru, just someone else to show them the way or give them permission, in a sense. I think a lot of people spend a lot of time spinning their wheels in analysis paralysis, instead of taking action and figuring it out for themselves.

Lastly, be adaptable. On your path to eight figures and beyond, the world is going to change a lot. You're going to change as a person. I started Pet Parents in January of 2016, so a little more than eight years now. In that time, I went from a twenty-something to a thirty-something, and my personal life as well as me as a human being and a man have changed. You grow. And that's inside of you, inside your direct control, which is far more in your control than your business, your employees, your industry, and of course, the external world.

Remember, everyone faces similar struggles, but those who stick with it are the ones who achieve their goals, whether it's losing weight, building muscle, or reaching eight figures and beyond. I hope you find these insights helpful. They've certainly been valuable in my own journey.

Hunter's doing great work by sharing content like this, and it can be incredibly useful. But always keep in mind that, ultimately, you're responsible for your own success. You have to continuously learn, improve your craft, and take action to make things happen. No one else can do it for you. Keep pushing forward, stay committed, and you'll be amazed at what you can achieve.

From the Bottom to the Top: Chase Roscher's Journey

I've been with my company for fifteen years, but it was started forty-six years ago. I started at the very bottom on salary making $40,000 a year, managing the crews, selling on the side, and just kind of worked my way up. Eventually, I bought 30 percent and then 35 percent to get to 65 percent, and then just bought the whole thing. So I've kind of learned it from the bottom and grown in it.

Let's start with the bad and the ugly, the lessons I've learned. Do everything with integrity. Treat everything like somebody is staring over your shoulder. Never invoice insurance for something you don't do. It always comes back. Never cut a corner, never decide to not put felt under a roof—guaranteed, that roof will have a leak, and they'll hire somebody else, who will find out. Don't put ice and water shield where it's code. Somehow, it always comes back to bite you.

Mistakes will happen. It's inevitable. It's contracting, it's roofing, it's construction. It's dirty. It's messy. There are a lot of inherent risks. You will make mistakes. Fix them. Don't argue, and don't try to charge when you've made a mistake. Just be honest up front and say, "We really screwed this up," and fix it. If you do that, that person will become a raving fan, and you will get way more out of them than the cost to fix it and make it right.

The stress is going to be overwhelming. You're going to carry a massive payroll. You're constantly expanding those horizons—and increasing the stress to pay those credit card bills to pay payroll. You go from being responsible for just your family, and as you start hiring people, you're responsible for fifteen families. The stress that you're going to carry is a heavy load. You have to talk about that. You can't just shoulder it.

Your spouse is not going to understand what's going on, why you feel the way you do, because from their perspective, maybe it's really successful. You're bringing home money, you're selling, and all is good. They don't understand the weight, so be open about that. Talk to them and explain that. Explain the money side of it, if it's something that they want to know and can comprehend. Sometimes spouses don't want to know that, they don't want to also shoulder the stress, but you have to figure out what they do want. You have to want to know what will help them to understand your situation, because when you're married, that's the focal point of the stress. They don't understand what you're going through, and so they think everything should be fine because the money's there when that's not always the case.

Be present. I know Hunter talks about this all the time, but be where your feet are when you're home. You have to find a way to disconnect. Set the phone down, be with your kids, be with your spouse. Find time to just pour into your family because as much as you're pouring into your business to help it grow, think about what would happen if you didn't pour into your business for growth.

For me, I'm not a big drinker. I never have been. I don't really do anything. I don't have any vices other than golf and good vacations, and that's what this life provides. Once you build it, you can take your kids anywhere in the world, and you don't have to think about it. I'm taking my kids to the Dominican for a week. Not a lot of people do that. I'm putting a pool in right now. There's not a lot of people that get to do that.

You also have the ability to help others achieve their dreams. I've got a couple of sales guys that never in their world would've thought that they could make well into six figures, $175,000, $200,000 a year. That's massive for me. That pushes me to want to help them and give them the opportunities to achieve their dreams.

One of the most rewarding aspects of success is the ability to give freely without expecting anything in return. It's incredibly fulfilling to be able to say, "Hey, here's a thousand bucks," or "Here's $5,000," to someone who's a good cause or struggling.

I had a kid who ran material for me. He'd only been with us for two months, but I could see his character. When he blew the motor in his car, I helped him through the process. I gave him a $2,000 down payment on a cheaper, but affordable vehicle. When he offered to pay me back, I refused. I told him, "I don't want you to pay me back, man."

That $2,000 wasn't much to me, but it was the world to this kid. And what it's done is create incredible loyalty. He's one of the greatest kids now. He'll do anything I ask because he knows I've got his back. I wouldn't have had that $2,000 to give if I didn't have a successful company.

This ability to give freely, without expecting a trade or keeping track, is truly freeing. It's not just about the money—it's about the impact you can have on someone's life, the loyalty you can build, and the good you can do when you're in a position to help. That's one of the most rewarding parts of building a successful business.

Always hire for your culture, not just because somebody's going to be productive; be slow to hire, quick to fire. That's something that I've learned and that has bit me in the butt so many times. Those are some of the key things I've learned working in this business, and I hope some of those nuggets are valuable to you as you go through your own journey.

Accelerating Growth With Speed and Precision:
Matt Ganzak's Journey

I own SaaS businesses, e-commerce businesses, and have consulted and partnered with some eight-figure brands, helping build them up from scratch. In my years of business development, I had my first seven-figure year in 2006, using mostly online marketing and internet marketing strategies to drive revenue. What I found in 2006 was that the only way to go from seven figures a year to eight figures and beyond was to work as part of a team where everyone efficiently, smoothly, and cohesively works together to progress business and move things forward.

In 2008, I took a job with one of the most visited websites at the time. They were struggling with some things and doing probably low eight figures a year. I ended up partnering with them to help grow their business, and we were able to turn things around. Within two to three years of working together, that business was able to double and even triple its size. All we had to do was put the right people in the right places and cut out the toxic behavior that was going on inside the brand.

What I learned by 2010 was that when we execute and put things together, the only way for us to grow the brand and the revenue is to work based upon our watch and not based upon a calendar. This means for every single project that we had, we would sit down as a team and say something akin to, "Okay, we're going to do this new landing page, we'll run this ad, we'll run it through this traffic source, and then we will get a report."

Once we had a game plan, we'd set people to work, having them put the landing pages together and then the ads. Then we would get the purchase order for the advertising traffic, and each team would do everything that day. So, if we have a meeting Tuesday morning at 9:00 a.m., then by 9:00 a.m. Wednesday morning everything needs to be done: the materials, the programming of the page, or at least staging for our website.

By getting what we needed done for a project in twenty-four hours, we were able to test more ideas and get them live faster. Sometimes they failed massively. I'm talking about investing $20,000 into the advertising just for it to fall flat. However, the next day we'd be testing something else, and we would make up for those losses. The biggest thing is we didn't have a loss of thirty days to deploy a campaign, which is how long it took before I joined their team. We only had a loss of twenty-four hours, allowing us the next day to focus and see what we needed to do better in order to fix things.

In the end, I helped the company toward an exit for multiple eight figures, and then I went on to launch several other brands. I've launched e-comm brands and SaaS platforms. I've also helped agencies scale. However, everything that I do is based upon the "use a watch, not a calendar" mindset.

Yes, it's painful, but it really weeds out the negative energy inside of your business. When you start using that sort of language with your team and say, "Tell me how long this is going to take," and then respond with, "I'm going to cut that time in half or cut it into a fourth to get it done," you are pressuring people to not only do things quicker, but think about things differently. Therefore, the end result ends up being exponentially better for the company because we learn something faster.

When we're developing software or a prototype, we program it to learn a single thing. I'll give you an example. On March 1st, I had an idea to have an app that told the user who was and wasn't engaging with their content on Facebook.

So, I reached out to my developer and said, "Hey, can we do this? Can you give me a prototype?"

He said, "Yeah, I'll have it for you in two weeks."

"Can you have the answer to me by tomorrow?" I asked.

He said, "Yeah, but it's not going to be pretty."

I told him, "I don't need it to be pretty. I just need to have an answer."

The next day, he said, "Yes, it's possible. Not only is it possible, but here is a working version of it that you can download and install into your Google Chrome where you can actually see it in action. Not that it is really doing or saving anything. I didn't have time to actually program that."

However, this was fine. I didn't need it to do the rest of that yet. Instead, I took a video, recorded it, and posted it to my Facebook, saying, "Hey, if I developed this app, would you guys want it?"

Over 2,000 people messaged in the comments, saying that they wanted it. So, we had the first alpha version of the app ready to go within two weeks, and within about seven days, we were getting the data and everything was in working order. Within another two weeks, I put it online for sale, and the guys were like, "Oh, it's going to take a while for me to build the subscription service and everything."

I said, "Just do a lifetime access and launch it."

I ended up making more money on launch day than the time and cost it took development to build the entire app. We went on to make seven figures from the app, and things just got better as we went forward. All because of the mindset of using your watch and not a calendar.

In the e-commerce business, it's wild. You can use AI to create mockups of products. If you don't know how to use the AI, you can just go to Upwork and hire somebody that can use the AI to create mockups. You could literally have an idea in the morning, and then by the afternoon, possibly have a mockup of a product. You could then put that product up on a landing page or a platform, drive traffic to it via Facebook ads, and be making sales by the time you go to bed. In other words, you don't have to have the product on hand to know whether or not there's actually a demand for it.

Then you can go back to those people and say, "Hey, sorry, we're having problems with fulfillment. Let me refund you, and give you this coupon where you can get a free product when the product actually comes in. I'll be sure to keep you updated." By doing things this way, you learn something within twenty-four hours, rather than spending years in development, years in product sourcing, and years in getting everything else set up and so-called perfect.

The lesson I learn in twenty-four hours is what's going to drive me to create successful brands. When I'm looking at creating an eight-figure brand, nine-figure brand from the ground up, I want to know if our assumptions are correct. If I can prove that assumption within twenty-four hours, then in thirty days I can create thirty different assumptions and test thirty different business ideas.

So, move fast, test fast, fail fast, and you'll be able to find that eight-figure, nine-figure brand. Then once you find what works, just put your foot on the throttle and accelerate as hard as possible.

Building an Eight-Figure Success From the Ground Up: Brandon Allen's Journey

My journey really began back in 2013, even before I started the business. It was when I decided to get out of debt, which planted a seed that allowed me to take the leap into entrepreneurship later.

My wife, Ashley, and I had about $60,000 in debt. We were both working normal low-paying jobs, making maybe $80,000 to $90,000 in the household between the two of us. We were renting, had car payments, tool payments—the bank would give me money, so I took out loans. We had credit cards, too. It was a big deal for us at the time.

I realized that between the two of us making that kind of money, even though it wasn't much, we shouldn't have been basically giving away the entire paycheck and not having anything left as soon as we got it. So we decided to get out of debt.

It took us two years of complete sacrifice. I was selling everything. I even sold my beloved motorcycle for a thousand bucks to this guy because I was yapping my mouth about my plan. I was like, "Yeah, man, I'm not going to have debt. I'm selling everything. I'm even going to sell my motorcycle." He offered me a thousand bucks on the spot, and I took it. Maybe that wasn't the smartest thing, but at the time, it didn't matter. That bike didn't matter. I wanted to be out of debt so that someday I could have whatever it was that I wanted.

After two years of paying off the debt, the third year we saved another $30,000 in the bank. That was the plan—pay off the debt, build an emergency fund, then buy a house, pay that off, and fifteen, twenty years down the road, we'd be living real good.

Meanwhile, my partner, Aaron, had been selling for different companies. Every so often he'd come to me and say, "Man, we need to start a business. We can do this. It's not that hard." I had a short run with a contracting company in the past and had a bad taste in my mouth. I thought it was scammy, not an honest way to make a living.

Finally, I told Aaron to either do something about it or shut up. He went out in 2014, sold his first book of business on his own—about $800,000. He came to me and said, "Look, I got the sales. We can do this." So I quit my job as a union operator, where I was making a pretty damn good living, and took the leap of faith.

I came in and did the operations part. Aaron was out selling. Anything from the sale to the signed contract was him; anything from the signed contract and beyond was me. We soon hired our very first sales rep, who I'm proud to say is still with us today.

I was about twenty-five when we started. I had just gotten out of debt, and had some money saved. For the first year of the business, I didn't take anything and actually burned through my entire savings account. But you know what? I never thought twice about it. I knew that we were onto something and that we didn't have a choice. It was going to work. I had seen plenty of other people make it work, and I thought, *If anybody can do this, Aaron and I can do this.*

When it comes to low points, it's really hard for me to remember them all. I think that's one of my strengths as a leader—I don't keep tabs on the bad things that happen. Sometimes that's bit me, where I do so much for people and don't keep track of it, and they take advantage.

But I can tell you this—all the low points had lessons in them, and I appreciate them for that. I've truly adapted that mindset. Even now, we're being investigated by the Department of Labor Wages and Hours Division. I didn't even know they existed until the other day when I got a letter. It's a huge deal, and I'm going through it, but right away I'm thinking, *Looks like we're about to learn a good lesson here.* Yes, it's going to cost a lot of money—the attorney alone is going to cost me $30,000 just to open the case. But we're going to be a better company because of it. We're going to learn a lot of things about compliance from this.

And secondly, we're even more valuable to somebody that comes in and wants to buy the business. When that person comes in, they see that we check the box for having a great safety program with OSHA and don't mess around. I look at it as just a step in becoming more and more valuable to someone that wants to come in and buy our business.

One thing that's been hard is losing friends as you grow. You're not going to get from one level to the next and continue to evolve without dropping some friends and changing the people you're around. That part kind of sucks because you care about these people, but you start to realize that if you continue to hang around these people, you're going to continue to get the same results.

I'm an organized person, but I'm not a genius. There's nothing extraordinary about my intelligence. But what I excelled at, and so did Aaron, was just having the tenacity to get up and come back at it. Even now, ten years in, there are still eighteen-hour days sometimes.

Back then, eighteen-hour days were common. It was all the time, almost every day. There were countless nights I stayed overnight in the office. I had a sleeping arrangement in this dumpy little thousand-square-foot office. I'd roll out my cotton sleeping bag and sleep for a couple hours, if I even slept. Sometimes you'd just keep working, and suddenly the sun's coming up, and your first employee comes in at seven with coffee, and you're like, "All right, here we go again, I guess."

The difference now is that those eighteen-hour days are my choice. When I'm spending a week in Bimini, then a week in Wisconsin, then off to Costa Rica, I'll cram everything into one long day at the office instead of wasting the whole week. I don't mind doing that because that's where I came from, and that's the freedom I have now.

We haven't really had a plateau in growth. We've had a very steady trajectory. It's been fairly damn consistent over the last decade—we'd have a year, then the next year we doubled, then maintained, then doubled again.

I think the most important thing as an entrepreneur is that the minute you're not required to have a little bit of balls, to have some courage in making a decision or taking that next step, you can pretty much guarantee you're not growing. We talk about the four Cs in our team meetings—commitment, courage, competence, and confidence. Courage is the most difficult part. That's where a lot of people fall out.

Some of the toughest decisions on the way to eight figures were changes in the team. Some of the first guys that were with us, that I thought would always be there, ended up really hurting our culture as we grew. They liked things the way they were and weren't willing to get uncomfortable and grow with us. Letting those people go—friends, lifelong friends, family members—was incredibly tough.

But here's one of the good stories: When I let one of our guys go almost a year ago, I told him, "Look, things are not working. We've talked about this for years. I think we've reached the end of the road. But I truly believe that if you start your own handyman business, you're going to be more fulfilled." I promised to support him every step of the way. Now, almost a year later, he's in a better place than he's ever been. He's got tens of thousands of dollars in the bank that he's earned for himself. He's happy. That's really amazing for me.

You can't be a victim. The world is not out to make your life easy for you. The world is out to make your life difficult. It's up to you to step on the side of that and not give it your attention and do what you're going to do anyway despite everything being in your way.

If you're aiming for eight figures, then focus on eight figures and don't stop. It's not going to be easy. The bigger you get, the more people are putting a target on your back, especially the government. You're going to get audits from everybody. Start off on the right foot. Don't wait three years to pay your first tax bill. Don't bypass getting all the proper insurance. Track all your wages. Be serious about safety stuff.

There are so many people out there who've reached a certain level of success and love to share their wisdom. Go talk to them, find those people, find yourself a mentor. But then actually take what they say seriously. Don't waste your time talking to them and then also waste time going through the BS they told you you could have avoided.

It's totally worth all the hard stuff, all the long hours, all the tough conversations. Being willing to do some of those things that most people aren't willing to do is the small stuff that can take you so far beyond what most people are able to achieve.

From IT Specialist to Roofing Mogul:
Randy Hurtado's Journey

I'm the chief operations officer and partner at DT Companies. Our story begins in 2016 when I joined DT Roofing. Prior to that, I was an IT security software specialist for twenty-four years, and I knew nothing about roofing or construction.

I came into this industry because the company I was contracting for got bought out for a hundred million dollars, and the new owners didn't need my services anymore. It kind of thrust me into this world. I would say I was desperate. God would say it was His plan.

I started with the company in sales and quickly learned that there wasn't much structure in place, especially when it came to technology. So I immediately reverted back to my IT background and started implementing tech solutions to support the organization. Along with selling, I began building a sales team.

2020 was a turning point for us. While many were losing jobs because of COVID, we saw an opportunity to find really good people without sales experience. That's exactly what we wanted—individuals with good moral ethics and integrity whom we could teach the DT way.

Our growth has been phenomenal. From a $1.8 million company in 2016, we're set to close over $40 million in revenue this year across our various companies, with $30 million coming from residential roofing alone. It's been a hard ride, but God has been with us throughout the entire process.

Our success has allowed us to expand beyond roofing. We now have a commercial roofing company, a construction company for homes and remodels, a garage door and service company, a gutter company, and an exterior cleaning company. These businesses not only feed off each other but also serve our community—including those who might be considered our competitors.

Today, we have seventy W2 employees across all companies, including thirteen residential salespeople and three commercial sales reps. We don't W2 our install crews, giving them the freedom to work for others when we're slow. I've learned that when you focus on just three or four crews and keep them as busy as possible, they'll run to the edges of the earth for you.

One major thing that's helped me to actually grow my own separate company outside of my partner with DT is another partnership I have with my buddy Ryan Van Fleet from Contractor Authority. Contractor Authority's largest product is roofingreferrals.com. Our success is rooted in relationship management. We do constant data analysis on where our leads come from, and 70 to 80 percent of our leads come from relationships our team has established with customers, professionals like real estate agents and insurance agents, and community involvement. While SEO, truck wraps, and billboards have made us money, nothing compares to the power of relationships. So I'd say relationship management is probably the most important asset, from a marketing standpoint, that you can spend money on.

The biggest struggle throughout this process has been dealing with the rapid growth. We've had very little turnover, and those we did let go, we helped find the career they needed with as much grace and mercy as possible.

Throughout this journey, we've never forgotten that our success comes from God. We pray that if we ever forget that, He'll take it all away. The moral of the story is: Treat everybody you work with as if they're the embodiment of Christ, and you'll always have people who treat you right.

Grit to Growth: Ty Backer's Unconventional Path to Roofing Success

I ended up in the roofing industry because I didn't really have anywhere else to go. I was twenty-three years old; my life was a mess. Addiction had taken its toll on me, I was on parole, and I decided I needed a geographical change. I ended up moving to York County, Pennsylvania, where my sister and brother-in-law lived. I saw that their lives had changed for the better, and it seemed like there was a lot more opportunity for someone like me as well, considering the fact that I had ruined every opportunity and burned every bridge back home. I honestly had nothing to lose. I was never able to gain anything with my troubles with the law and being hooked on drugs at a very young age. I couldn't even get a driver's license until age twenty-five because of many underage drinking arrests.

Shortly after arriving in York County, my brother-in-law and his best friend decided to start a siding business. They showed me everything from the installation, product management, and operations. I owe everything I have today to them for giving me the opportunity and another chance at life. I didn't know it then, but this was just the beginning of what was to come for me. I realized later that I needed to make all of the mistakes in order to become the person I am today. Through pain comes growth, and being the knucklehead I am, I needed to experience a lot of self-inflicted pain. I came from a long line of carpenters. My dad is a mechanical engineer by trade but also a great carpenter. His dad and brothers are all master carpenters. So, I have always been good with my hands, and thankfully mechanically inclined with street smarts, considering I graduated from school while in Franklin County Prison at the age of seventeen.

Needless to say, after many years, I decided to leave in late 2007 and started my own company. Working with family can be complicated. In any family business, there are many perspectives: his, mine, and the truth. This dynamic definitely shapes our business practices today, influences how we view our industry and our competitors, and affects the treatment of our co-workers. I was single and full of resentment, and that almost killed me. July 7th, 2008, TC Backer Construction was established. My resentment drove me for a while, and my behaviors were not the greatest in my personal life. By early 2010, the company grew to a few million dollars. From the outside, everything looked great, but I was dying on the inside. I was no longer taking care of myself spiritually. The principles that helped me get sober were no longer on my radar. I was so obsessed with work, and I was absolutely killing myself. I ended up relapsing. This in itself could be an entire book. Things were rough for about nine months, but I was able to pull myself together on August 16, 2010.

Again, some more pain was needed in order for me to grow. I honestly believe I needed to come that close to losing everything in order for me to learn, achieve, and appreciate the things that I have today. I'm not talking about the material things. Chasing the money almost killed me or locked me up for a long time. It's funny how God works. At the time, I thought I ruined and lost everything again. God only removed all of my "wants" and ended up leaving me everything I needed. He removed all of the stressful things in my life. The principles that got me sober, "God, AA, and Everything Else," were put back into perspective. I had it all backward prior to going back out again. It was "Everything Else, Sometimes God, and No AA." I learned real quick that anything I put in front of God or AA I will lose. Another lesson was learned.

Only this time, I had to earn it. It didn't seem like it came to me as easy as it did the first time. Business was slow; we were in the middle of the Great Recession. Obviously, I wasn't planning for the future very well, my vision was clouded, I was filled with guilt, and lost my license again for another four years. I wasn't going to give up. I paid someone to drive me to all of the appointments, to the jobs and any meetings I had. It was a humbling time of my life. After all of that, I met my wife, Jana. We actually met years before and knew each other well. After a year of just talking, we decided to actually start dating. Honestly, we decided to come out of the closet and tell her parents that we were dating. Shortly after that, she moved in, and I convinced her that it would be a good idea to come work with me.

2011 to 2012 marked a profound transformation in both my personal and professional life. The clarity of the business vision began to crystallize as I faced personal challenges, including my mother's second battle with cancer and significant changes in business insurance laws encompassing health insurance, workers' compensation, and general liability.

During this period, Jana was fully immersed in the business. However, as my mother's condition required increasing care, we faced a pivotal decision. Jana chose to step back from her professional role to devote herself to my mother's care full-time. Concurrently, we were at a crossroads with our business model, needing to decide whether to continue contracting our staff as 1099 subcontractors, which would require them to manage their own insurance needs, or to transition them to W-2 employees. This decision was complicated by new insurance legislation that could subject us to audits. The latter option was financially daunting, as it would increase our operational costs significantly.

After many sleepless nights and prayerful consideration, we chose to transition our team to W-2 employment. This was not an easy task. Everyone enjoyed the immediate cash flow, but transitioning meant potentially reduced take-home pay due to tax implications. To offset this, we decided to raise our teammates' wages to match their net income, ensuring they did not feel the financial shift.

This decision eventually proved to be less challenging once we considered the long-term benefits for our company and our co-workers, particularly in terms of safety and health. Providing workers' compensation meant that any injured co-worker would be adequately covered, and unemployment benefits would support anyone laid off because of work shortages. This planted a seed. We felt how great it would be to offer health insurance. So Jana and I decided to go on a mission and do whatever it took to be able to offer benefits. Let me remind you, things were tight. There were weeks that went by that we couldn't pay ourselves. We spent a lot of nights lying in bed worrying how we were going to pay our bills. Or we were stressed out about having too much work and figuring out how to get it all done. We kept chipping away at it until eventually, in 2016, we felt we were financially stable enough to offer medical, dental, and optical insurance. That was, at the time, the second biggest milestone of my career.

Following the successful integration of health insurance, our next goal was to establish a retirement plan. By 2019, we had rallied our team and were ready to choose between offering an IRA or a 401(k); the majority preferred the latter. Unfortunately, the onset of the pandemic in early 2020 forced us to pause these plans, as Pennsylvania shut down. However, we doubled our efforts in marketing and not only sustained our business but also expanded it significantly within two years. Again, it's funny how God works. Our company, at that time, had hit a plateau, and we were supposed to close our doors because of COVID. We choose to stay open and eventually get our exemption paperwork to stay open. It seemed like we were the only roofing company open and doing inspections. We blew up and doubled down, and gained tons of market share. Everyone else was backing off, and we were killing it. With my head clear at this point, I knew this wasn't going to last forever. We quickly prepared ourselves for another recession. I figured if it didn't happen, no big deal, but I wasn't going to let what happened to us in 2010 happen again. So, we paid down our debt and stayed liquid. We went from low eight figures to mid eight figures. We literally doubled our revenue.

By late 2021, we were able to launch our 401(k) plan, adjust salaries to match inflation, and provide a company match to their contributions, ensuring their financial growth without risk. This initiative was so unprecedented that even our bank was astounded by our commitment.

This isn't about boasting of our achievements but about underscoring an investment in our team who remained with us through the pandemic. And some have been with us since the beginning. This experience solidified our resolve and helped fortify our company culture, focusing not just on financial success but on creating an environment where co-leaders and co-workers feel valued, heard, and empowered. Our aim has always been to build a company that not only strives for excellence but also nurtures a community where everyone wants to belong.

Today I am the co-owner, founder, and CEO of TC Backer Construction, Horizon Lawns, TCB Rentals, and Rocket Group, and I oversee a diverse portfolio of companies. I am also the co-founder and co-producer of the *Behind the Toolbelt* podcast. My wife, Jana, whom I call the "Chief Everything Officer," is my rock, managing both our home and the upheavals life throws our way. Together, we've raised three remarkable children and now enjoy spending time with our three delightful grandchildren.

As a CEO/founder of a rapidly expanding roofing company, I found out my role was crucial in driving growth, ensuring operational efficiency, and maintaining a strategic vision. You will need to create a clear vision, mission, and goals for the company and teams. It is going to be crucial for guiding your teams and ensuring alignment with your strategic and tactical objectives.

One of the most important things is helping individuals grow, not always thinking about growing the business and revenue, but more importantly, focusing on your teams and people's growth. Some entrepreneurs can't handle getting out of the limelight. Their ego and pride get in the way of other people's growth. I'm speaking from experience. When this happens, the company's growth stops, or even worse, you start to lose good people. Don't be afraid to surround yourself with smart people within your organization. Stay humble and find humility. Business isn't always about growing the business. It's about giving people opportunities. It's about having a dream big enough for other people's dreams to fit in. It's about building a company that people want to work for, creating a culture people want to be a part of, having an organization that other organizations aspire to be! When the people grow, the business will grow. The sooner you learn that this isn't about you, never was, the better. The real flex isn't revenue; it's the impact on people's lives. The amount of people you can touch in your lifetime before we leave this earth. Roofing is only the vehicle that allows us to do so. Put in the work. Develop yourself. Then you'll be able to develop others.

Be prepared for people to think you're crazy, but don't let those people's opinions affect your judgment or distract you from wanting to accomplish great things. Daring things. Don't let their fears hold you back. If we are not willing to take risks and bet on ourselves, then who will? Don't let the outside environment influence your situation. People who you thought were your friends may resent your success. Not everyone will see the things you do, and that's fine. They don't need to be in your circle. Search out people that will help level you up. Continuously keep pushing. Never stop learning, and remain teachable.

Scaling the Summit: Lance Bachmann's Unwavering Path to Digital Dominance

When I started 1SEO, I was leaving AT&T, where I was running a team of 900 people at the time. I was nervous, scared, not sure what to do. I said to myself, "Man, if I could just take it day by day and get through a few months." Jackie Eldridge, David DePaolo, and Jolin came with me. We started selling and figuring things out.

After probably a year in, I thought to myself, *Okay, we have a business here. A real business.* We had a few other people working for us, a developer or two. I started thinking about how to scale this thing. We went through some bad people and people that took advantage. I was a terrible leader at times, and the self-doubt that kicks in and the anxiety at those points, it's tough.

It was probably year two as we were grinding through it. We decided to move our in-home business into an actual office, and then we started hiring more people. It was at this time when I decided if we were going to do this, I had to be able to lead 24/7. You have to be a constant leader.

I think there are two types of leaders: There are leaders that think their title makes them a leader, and then there are leaders that actually don't care about the title. I've never had a title for that reason. My thought is that I've got to show, by my actions, that I'm willing to outwork everyone, and that I'm invested in my team.

That's where I started seeing the most movement of the people, and we went from two people to forty people over the next few years.

Truth be told, there were ups and downs, taking on debt at times, but not much, because I lived debt-free.

My first year in business, I only made $6,700. My second year, I think I only made $30-some thousand, and then I went to around $80,000. So I lived a very modest life; I lived off my savings from AT&T.

When we got to about thirty people, I knew I needed a CEO. I knew we needed an office that represented us. I was paying $8,000 a year in just property tax on my building that I'd bought for $185,000 and paid off. I went and leased a space in this building—it was beautiful—for $22,000 a month.

I remember everyone thought I was nuts. The building was paid off, but I said, "Man, if we're going to grow and we're going to show that we're the elite agency in the country, you just gotta go all in."

That was a defining moment. Everyone bought into 1SEO. They saw I went all in, so all my employees started going all in, and all my leaders went all in. There was a turning point when I showed Bill Rossell, my CEO (who's still my CEO of LB Capital) the building and what we were doing, and he went all in. He knew I wasn't playing. He quit his job and came back with me.

I did grow 1SEO to over one hundred employees, and I sold it to a private equity firm, which I've totally exited out of now. I've sold multiple companies now.

The biggest piece of advice I can give everyone as you go through this: You have to get rid of the distractions. Whether it be your family, your friends, haters, and doubters—whoever it is. They don't even understand your dream and what you're trying to achieve. They can't comprehend having that kind of freedom. Remember this: Everyone's going to come to you with something. They always have a motive.

They always have some bias, some self-interest. There's going to be leaders far and in between that can separate their bias and their self-interest. So you have to have open eyes to everything.

You have to be so focused; everything has to be focus driven to the point where it's all that matters. You almost have to be obsessed with it. People say, "Have a work-life balance," but you can't at the beginning. When I went all in, I was just obsessed with it. Yes, I saw my children, and I worked. I stopped going to the bar, and I stopped drinking all the time. I did all that when I was younger.

Learn how to read a P&L inside and out. That was the changing point in my whole entire career. P&Ls, cash flow, balance sheets—understand the actual trends. That will get you in the end.

There's going to be a lot of ups and downs. Stay focused, stay true to you, be authentic, and you're going to see a lot of positive things.

Unwavering Resolve: Tom Shipley's Persistent Climb to Business Excellence

As an entrepreneur, you will have times when your business hits a wall that feels like a concrete building crushed it. Your team and advisors tell you you are done. This is where successful entrepreneurs know that it is never as bad as everyone thinks it is, and there is always a potential solution. It's all about resourcefulness!

From a very young age, I knew I was going to be an entrepreneur owning and leading multiple businesses. But what did that actually mean? Initially, it wasn't very clear to me.

My entrepreneurial journey truly began after I got out of the Army. I served in the special forces and returned to the States with just $100 in my pocket. During my time overseas, I saw a product that sparked my interest. When you've served in the military, your perspective on risk changes dramatically. While fear is always present, when you aren't risking your life, you have the luxury of betting on yourself and taking massive leaps of faith. That's exactly what I did to start my first company—found a product, found a manufacturer, and just went for it. There wasn't a door I did not go through to ensure success. Most important is that every business you have is your greatest learning experience.

Whether you're at eight figures or nine figures in your business, the real question is: How do you maintain it? Over my entrepreneurial career, I see it as navigating a series of mountain ranges. You reach various peaks, but you're only at the summit with the wind at your back for fleeting moments. Most of the time, it's rough climbs up, difficult descents down. Occasionally, you fall off the side of the cliff and hope you survive.

Let me share this with you: There were numerous times when my company hit a brick wall. Several of my companies hit concrete walls. Everyone around me said the company was done. My board advisor recommended shutting it down. In those moments, true entrepreneurs show their grit and tenacity. We just don't quit. Occasionally, we analyze the data and have to pivot, but it's not in our nature to give up. Grit, tenacity, and resourcefulness are in our DNA.

I want to give you some context about the low moments in business. One instance was when I merged my first large business—my passion—with another business. I'd gone all in, even sacrificing significant time with my little girls. But a year after the merger, I was out. Most of my employees were let go. My businesses were kept for parts they could leverage. I was left with significant debt, no resources, and two little girls at home. During these periods, you just have to get scrappy, figure out a way to bring in dollars, and then regroup for the next big opportunity. Within three years of launching my next brand, we generated over $100 million in revenue and, over its life, did over $1 billion.

The key for entrepreneurs is understanding that failure is just a matter of definition. Great founders have had multiple failures that taught them the lessons they needed for that big opportunity. The worst thing I suffered after that first failed merger was shame—shame I didn't have to lean into but just didn't know any better. Along the way, we as entrepreneurs will experience failures in our businesses. We'll even have failed businesses. That doesn't mean we're failures. These are the greatest lessons that form the foundation to reach the next level.

I remember my first business—the question was: How do I get to $1 million? My second business—how do I get to $10 million? My third business—how do I get to $100 million, which we did within three years, and then how do we sustain annual revenue of over $100 million? We built our infrastructure to support us at that level. Whether it's the successes or failures, they help raise our expectations and give us the tools to reach the next level.

Let me tell you about another low point. My partner and I had a business doing between $70 to $100 million a year consistently for about seven or eight years. We had offers to acquire the business between $55 and $75 million. It was exciting until we got a phone call from our sole source, the only FDA-approved manufacturer for our biggest continuity product, responsible for 85 percent of our revenue. This $500 million manufacturer went out of business—chapter seven, locks on the door, no access to our products, components, or supply chain. We knew it would take eighteen months to get our own FDA approval. It was a subscription business, and if you don't ship to your customers within thirty to sixty days, you quickly lose your subscribers, which is what happened. We watched our profit go from $650,000 a month to losing $600,000 a month within six months, and then our senior lender said they were calling our loan and wanted us to liquidate.

But here's what I learned: Even in those moments, there's always hope and opportunity. So, we got to work buying one week at a time. Our team came together, rose to the challenge, and this was my favorite year, growing back to $650K per month in profit.

Successful entrepreneurs get comfortable with a level of stress that would break most people. We've had enough ups and downs, failures, and gotten through enough brick walls that we develop confidence in our ability to navigate out of the most challenging. No matter how difficult the problem, this too shall pass, and we'll soon be on the other side of it.

When you're at the top of the hill, it's never as good as you think. There's always some looming dark cloud. But also, when you're at the edge of the cliff, it's never as bad as you think. There are always options.

The final lesson to share is that the most important thing is the "who." Not just finding the who with the answer or the who is on your team, but who is in your life that makes the journey worthwhile. No matter how difficult it is, I learned the most important investment is to steal time and invest every day in those most important things around you. Businesses come and go; family doesn't. Our responsibility is to make every chapter in our epic novel spectacular living by our rules. We own the rules and own the game.

Raising the Bar: John Franco's Defiant Climb in Roofing

I've been in this game for about seven years now, operating at over $10 million, averaging $13 million a year for the past three or four years. Let me tell you, it has not been easy.

If somebody came to me today and said they wanted to start a roofing company, especially in this day and age, I'd definitely tell them, "Good luck. Don't give up. Focus on your goals." But I'd also warn them to plan on working sixteen, eighteen, twenty hours a day, running multiple jobs at once, and wearing multiple hats because that's exactly what I did.

People don't see it now because I have a team of great managers, staff, and sales reps that run my operation 80 to 90 percent of the time consistently, and they get it done. But before that, there were a lot of long nights, sacrifices, marriage struggles, and kid struggles. I didn't get to spend a lot of time with my children. There was a lot of grit and sacrifice that led to where I'm at today, which allows me the time and financial freedom I have now.

Let me take you back to the beginning. I started with just $20,000 and a dream of owning my own roofing company. I wanted to set the standards correctly, get away from the known roofing contractor ways and scammers out there. I wanted to do something different, and I believe I've reached that goal. But the only way I was able to was by creating a standard that I thought was right and needed to be changed in this industry.

So I went ahead with that $20,000 and started the company. I quickly realized I needed way more than that, but I was going to give it a shot anyway. Storms came through—we're in Florida, great opportunity—

and we started making money. But man, there were times when I had to beg suppliers to release orders because we didn't have any money to pay them. We were probably over $100,000 in debt, more jobs to build than contractors sold, and not any money to pay the supplier.

That was one moment where I thought this ship was going to sink. Fortunately, checks started rolling in. It's like they say, "Don't give up. Just keep going. Do your best." Luckily, I had built relationships with the suppliers, and one thing I can say is: Build those relationships. Keep those relationships clean. Do the next right thing. Be transparent with your vendors, suppliers, and anybody in your network because you never know when one day they're going to help you out.

There were other challenging moments too. I remember a house burning down three hours after we torched the roof. I thought, "There it is again. We're done." But by the grace of God, the fire marshal who came in said there was an electrical shortage inside the house where the lady's nightstand was. It had nothing to do with us. Again, we kept moving forward through the good, the bad, and the ugly. I just didn't stop.

And here we are now, operating at $13 million. Hire the right people—they handle all that crazy stuff. I don't have to handle those stressful situations anymore. We've been running at a good full speed ahead at $13 million, and we're looking to do $20 million. It's all because of having the right people in place. I don't get to work *in* my business anymore like I did for many years. Now I get to work *on* my business.

One thing I could say is I grew up in an environment where every day was a real struggle, every day was a heartache. It seemed like it was never going to end. And here I am, living a life beyond my wildest dreams. So no matter how hard it got for me in the beginning, I just kept going because nothing stunned me. I've been through some hard times. This wasn't hard. This might have been exhausting, this might have been a sacrifice of moments that I could have had, but in the end, it's well worth it.

I'm glad to be here. Hopefully, we'll do $20 million within the next year or two. That's the goal. We're going to keep rocking and rolling.

Words of Encouragement

As we conclude this journey through *Unlocking 8 Figures: The Roadmap to $10M*, I want to emphasize that our intention has been to provide you with everything you need to reach eight figures and beyond while maintaining profitability and having fun. The strategies, frameworks, and insights shared in this book are your toolkit for extraordinary success.

There's one element I want to touch on again: I can't stress enough the power of *community*. Surrounding yourself with individuals who are either striving for similar goals or have already achieved them can be the difference in winning or losing. That's why I want to invite you to join us at one of our events or become part of our leadership community, Revolt.

If you're looking for a more hands-on approach, we're here to help. Whether you're interested in joining our community or exploring one-on-one coaching, don't hesitate to reach out. We offer various services tailored to support your entrepreneurial journey. Simply head over to TheRevolt.com/community and request more information.

Remember, you don't have to be anyone special to build a company that generates over $10 million a year. Your past, no matter how rough, doesn't define your future. What matters is the work you're willing to put in and the vision you cast for the team members who believe in you. By following the plan laid out in this book and committing to your goals, you can create a life beyond your wildest dreams. Not only that, but you'll be in a position to provide opportunities for your team members and give back to your community.

For those looking to dive deeper into leadership and legacy, I recommend checking out my *Wall Street Journal* #1 Bestseller, *Make It Count*, that includes a foreword written by my friend, John C. Maxwell. It's available in hardcopy or on Audible for those who prefer to listen.

Thank you for taking the time to read *Unlocking 8 Figures*. If you found value in these pages, I encourage you to share it with others who might benefit. Don't forget to explore our resource section, where you'll find links to all the tools I've mentioned throughout this book. These resources are designed to help you continue growing your company and your legacy.

Remember, the path to eight figures is about more than just financial success. It's about personal growth, creating value, and making a lasting impact. You have the power to transform not only your life but also the lives of those around you and for the generations that will come after you. Now, armed with the knowledge from this book, it's time to take action and turn your entrepreneurial dreams into reality.

I'm rooting for you.

To your success,

Hunter Ballew

RESOURCES

TheRevolt.com/roadmap

1. Monday.com Setup (Chapter 3: Structured for Success)
2. Job Profitability Sheet (Chapter 4: Financial Fundamentals)
3. *Clarity Calculator* (Chapter 5: Strategic Clarity & Chapter 12: The Path Forward)
4. Recruiting Funnel (Chapter 6: Recruiting Top Talent)
5. DFY Recruiting Service (Chapter 6: Recruiting Top Talent)
6. The *Six-Figure Blueprint* (Chapter 7: Train and Retain)
7. Lead Tracking Sheet (Chapter 8: Levers of Scale)
8. *Seven-Figure Handshakes* Spreadsheet (Chapter 8: Levers of Scale)
9. "Why Cornerstone" Example Video (Chapter 9: Mastering Sales)
10. Virtual Assistant Service (Chapter 8: Levers of Scale & Chapter 10: Winners Focus on Winning)

www.ingramcontent.com/pod-product-compliance
Lightning Source LLC
Chambersburg PA
CBHW071713120626
46550CB00001B/210